# THE RELATIONSHIP BETWEEN TRUST, COMMITMENT, AND

# LEADER ACTIONS WITH INTENT TO LEAVE

# THE UNITED STATES ARMY

**J. Andrew Forsyth, Ph.D.**

**2016**

# THE RELATIONSHIP BETWEEN TRUST, COMMITMENT, AND LEADER ACTIONS WITH INTENT TO LEAVE THE UNITED STATES ARMY

J. Andrew Forsyth, Ph.D.

## Abstract

Trust in military leadership is increasingly a problem of confidence and commitment, a phenomenon documented in detail within the 2014 Quadrennial Defense Review (QDR), published as a means of developing a strategic plan for military readiness. Several research studies show trust in leadership is arguably among the most important variables in relation to intent to leave an organization (Milligan, 2003). Trust continues to be a key factor in commitment within the military (Vadell, 2008). The problem in this research is the perceived lack of trust that officers hold with their leadership. The combination of senior leaders losing confidence in captains and the growing doubts about the trustworthiness of senior military leaders creates a knowledge gap in trust, explained in this research. The knowledge gap is seen when there is a lack of credibility with senior leadership as a result of diminished levels of trust from captains. Previous research suggested that the lack of trust and commitment impact intentions to leave. The purpose of this study was to examine the relationship between trust, commitment, leader actions, and intent to leave the military. Analyzing numerical survey data from 362 captains, the ultimate goal was to examine the relationships between trust, commitment and leader actions. The rationale behind this study; having a better understanding of the concept of trust and its relationship to retention, may have implications for future leader development and overall military readiness. This study utilized Milligan's theory as the foundation, as applied to trust in military leadership. Research findings conclude with

Tables 29-31 and the following points: *trust* is a growing factor in leadership and thought to be part of the reasoning behind officers leaving the Army; there exists a significant statistical relationship between *trust* and *intent to leave*; *trust* is directly related to the intent for officers' leaving the Army; there is a statistically significant relationship between *commitment* and *intent* of officers leaving the Army; *leader action* was a statistically insignificant predictor to *intent to leave*. Final implications suggest that with an increase of *trust* and *commitment* in leadership there is a decreased intention to leave the military.

## BIOGRAPHICAL SKETCH

John Andrew Forsyth is a native of Rochester, New York. He holds a Bachelor of Science degree from Rochester Institute of Technology, New York, an MBA and Ph.D. in Educational Leadership from Trident University, Cypress California.

John served as an active duty Soldier for more than twenty-five years and held numerous military assignments as an enlisted Soldier serving in Germany and Bosnia; as an Officer, he commanded Bravo Company 210 Brigade Support Battalion, 10th Mountain Division in both Iraq and Fort Drum. He also served as the Battalion Executive Officer of the largest Sustainment Battalion in Europe and is a graduate of the Army's Command and General Staff College.

This book is dedicated to a former commander, Orlando D. Critzer. Of all the factors and constructs of successful leadership that can be assembled and studied, the ones that you imparted me with will last a lifetime. This research revolves around the constructs of trust, commitment, and leader actions. After conducting the research, it was personally obvious that the most influential attributes came from trust and commitment in relation to an intention to leave the Army.

Bosnia, 1996, as a company commander, you led the company from the front in every conceivable fashion; something I carried forward with me to the best of my ability through my company command time and will carry with me for the remainder of my time in the military. I thank you for the inspiration you gave me at the most influentially critical time in my life. Your trust as a leader inspired me to carry the torch you lit for me, subsequently, the torches I lit along the way which have circled back to guide me through the completion of this research project. Great leadership is not easily forgotten.

**BANDITS NEVER QUIT!**

**BNQ**

# ACKNOWLEDGMENTS

I would like to extend my utmost gratitude to Dr.'s Wenling Li and Khallid Shabazz who served as my committee members. A special appreciation humbly goes to Dr. Pamela Wilson who served as my committee chair. I thank her profoundly for her patience, flexibility, and recommendations that resulted in this final product. I could not have made it without all of the combined support and mentoring. An extra special thank you goes to Dr. Wenling Li, for playing a dual role as committee member as well as the Director of the Ph.D. Program. Her flexibility towards my academic needs was instrumental in the successful program completion.

I would like to dedicate this research project to my two sons Larz and Kayn. Many times my work-related studies took away time we could have spent together. I thank you for your understanding and dedication to my education goals and allowing me to achieve this milestone. Life-long learning is an essential part of growing, as learning never ends. Best of luck on your journey!

A heartfelt special thank you to Tamra Garfield-Lemay for being such an amazing person and for helping me reach this milestone. Since childhood, you have always been there for me. I am extremely proud of the wonderful person you are and the "attack!" attitude you instilled in me. Had it not been for you and the help you offered when it was most needed, I certainly would not have been successful in completing this book and am forever in your debt!

Table of Contents

CHAPTER 1. INTRODUCTION

CHAPTER 2. LITERATURE REVIEW

CHAPTER 3. RESEARCH METHODOLOGY

LIST OF TABLES

# LIST OF FIGURES

# LIST OF ABBREVIATIONS

Military Occupational Specialty - MOS

Brigade Combat Team - BCT

Combat - Direct front line operations

Combat Support - MOS in support of frontline combat operations

Sustainment - MOS which provide logistical support to the Combat operations

OPTEMPO – Operational Tempo

**Military Officer Rank:**

O1 - Second Lieutenant (2LT)

O2 - First Lieutenant (1LT)

**O3 - Captain (CPT)**   ---*Research Study Population Group*---

O4 – Major (MAJ)

O5 - Lieutenant Colonel (LTC)

O6 - Colonel (COL)

O7 - Brigadier General (BG)

O8 - Major General (MG)

O9 - Lieutenant General (LTG)

O10 - General (GEN)

# LIST OF TERMS

*Commander* - A person commanding over a specific unit and its members (Mish, 1996).

*Commission* - An official certificate issued by the government conferring rank as an officer in the U.S. armed forces (Mish, 1996).

*Leadership* - A process whereby an individual influences others to achieve a common goal (Northouse, 2004).

*Military Service* - This represents active full-time participation in one of the five United States armed forces branches: Army, Air Force, Coast Guard, Marines, and Navy.

*Officer* - A commissioned military member in a position of authority, (Mish, 1996).

*Organizational Commitment* - A psychological state that: (a) characterizes the employee's relationship with the organization, and (b) has implication for the decision to continue or discontinue membership in the organization (Meyer, Allen, & Smith, 1993).

*Organizational Trust* - The confidence that employees give to management and the degree to which they believe what management tells them (Sashkin, 1996).

*Professional Military Education (PME)* - This comprises specific military courses that incorporate military history, organization, serving missions and command authority.

*Rank* - *This* represents an official grade or position designating authority (Mish, 1996).

*Captain* - The rank of captain is normally achieved after four years of active duty service. The initial commitment is completed and the member then has the opportunity to leave the military.

*Army leader* - one who by virtue of assigned responsibility inspires and influences people to accomplish organizational goals.

CHAPTER 1. INTRODUCTION

Introduction

*Trust* in leadership is the center-of-gravity within the United States Army Profession. As the U.S. Army transitions from an era of substantial operational deployments to an era characterized by preparing the force for the next series of conflicts, it faces several threats to trust. An environment of reduced force structure and fiscal austerity will accompany the current transition. How the Army profession fares in the coming decade will be based on the trust the institution engenders among its members and with the American people.

A 2008 report on American military cultures, The Center for Strategic and International Studies (CSIS) suggests that to be effective in the twenty first century, the Department of Defense must explore new patterns of leadership and command relationships; a recommendation that suggests that transforming leadership will be a significant part of the DOD's transformation strategy.

Consistent with a 2011 U.S. Army Center for Army Leadership report which concluded, "…trust is a strategic advantage for the Army." Further analysis over the course of the campaign established trust as an essential characteristic of the Army Profession. To achieve trust in the profession, by its members, requires a sustained relationship of trust among the members of the profession and its cohorts. Member trust in the Army, as an institution, is based on the relationship between members and the profession's senior leaders, as well as perceptions of the organizational bureaucracy that operationalizes those senior leaders' actions.

The Department of the Army-directed Profession of Arms (PoA) campaign emphasized trust as an essential characteristic of the Army Profession along with military expertise, honorable service, and stewardship of the profession. The PoA campaign began in 2011 under the leadership of GEN Martin Dempsey, commander of Training and Doctrine Command (TRADOC). When Dempsey became the 37th chief of staff of the Army, his initial guidance to the force stressed trust, discipline, and fitness as the three areas that he would discuss with commanders during visits around the Army. His successor, GEN Ray Odierno, in his "Initial Thoughts" and his "Marching Orders", appropriately labelled trust as "the bedrock of our honored profession" (See Figure 1).

In the most recent (2014) Quadrennial Defense Review (QDR) the Department of Defense (DOD) calls for a complete paradigm shift in conducting Army business. The Department's newest transformation strategy is designed to ensure the preeminence of the U.S. military well into the 21st century. This leadership transformation will require the recruitment and retention of a committed force with highly developed technical skills and the ability to lead in the complex environment of the future.

"The leader development and talent management systems we have today are not adequate to produce the Army Professionals required for tomorrow," John McHugh, current Secretary of the Army. Producing these professionals demands a comprehensive Human Dimension Strategy oriented on the individual, the team and the institution. This investment in the human dimension is a foundational component of the Army's comprehensive strategy known as Force 2025 and Beyond to change the Army and deliver land power as a strategic instrument of the future Force.

As recognized by GEN Odierno, "we must optimize the human performance of every Soldier in the Army and build cohesive teams of trusted professionals who thrive in ambiguity and chaos." The newly implemented *Army Human Dimension Strategy*

*(AHDS) of 2025* brings together multiple Army efforts and reframes those efforts within the context of current emerging requirements. Implementation of the AHDS is essential to the future *Force 2025 and Beyond*. A key concept underpinning this strategy is first and foremost, the Army must develop cohesive teams of trusted professionals that thrive in ambiguity and chaos.

Trust can be considered a primary attribute associated with successful leadership. Managerial and leadership effectiveness is, more than ever, dependent upon the ability to gain the trust of followers (Brockner et al., 1997). As a result, employees monitor the organizational environment as a means of assessing whether to place trust in management or not. Therefore, organizational processes are sometimes believed to communicate management's view of its employees. If the physical traits of an organization, such as structures and command climate, communicate distrust in employees by the management, it is believed that employees will respond with distrust. Figure one shows *trust* as one of the Army's strategic advantages and an essential characteristic of the Army Profession.

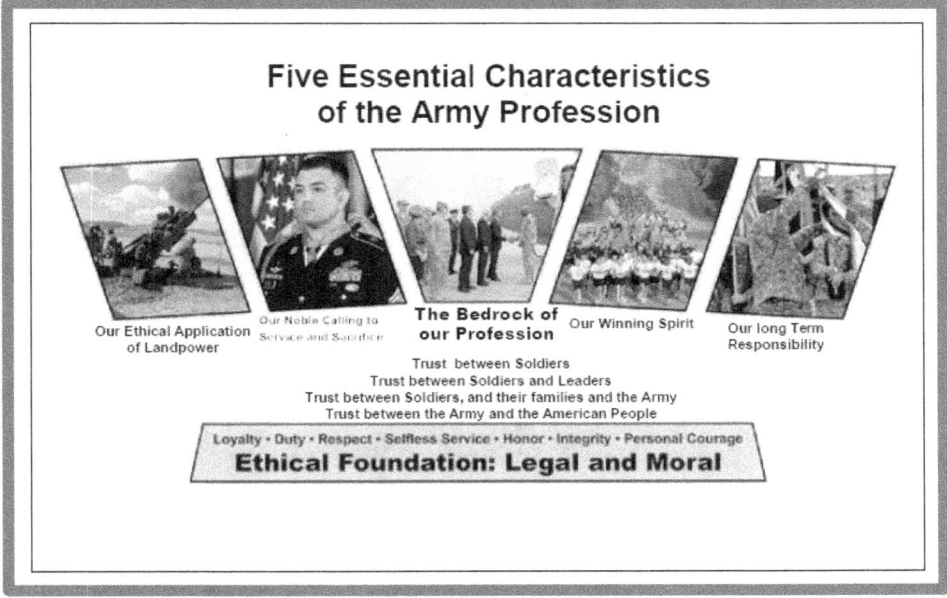

**Figure 1. Characteristics of the Army Profession**

## Defining Trust

Trust is a "collective attribute" based upon the relationships between people that exist in an organization, (Luhmann, 1979). Systems or organizational trust's primary effect is the reduction of social complexity and the increased tolerability of uncertainty in external relationships. Within organizations, trust contributes to more effective implementation of strategy, greater managerial coordination (McAllister, 1995), and more effective work teams (Doney, Cannon, & Mullen, 1998). Trust is a learnable, measurable skill that makes organizations more profitable, people more promotable and relationships more energizing, (Covey, 2013). Vadell (2008) explains that senior leadership's investment in their captains is embedded within the operational definition of trust.

Perry and Mankin (2007) both argued the potential for creating trust lies within the organizations capability to influence the internal quality of life and their ability to strengthen employee performance. Without trust, the world becomes an undesirable and unpleasant place. While there is no universally accepted definition of trust, many scholars have evaluated the relevance of predictability and confidence in generating trust. Because we have needs that require the services of other people, trust can be defined as an individual's reliance upon another, under conditions of dependence and risk, (Kipnis, 1998).

Milligan (2003) proved how previous research on trust in leadership and trust in employees impacted organizational commitment. Vadell (2008) explored trust in U.S. Air Force leadership and an airman's intent to leave the military. The current study utilizes Milligan's findings and examines organizational trust, commitment and leader actions as it pertains to an intention to leave the military. This findings of this study offer a better understanding of the concept of trust and its relationship to officer retention in the U.S. Army, which may have implications for future leadership development efforts and improved overall military readiness. The overall purpose of this study examined current organizational trust in Army leadership and how it affects captains' intent to leave military service.

The threat of losing trust within an organization is compounded by corrosion of the professional identity within the segment of the Army officer corps, entering its tenure as senior leaders. As stewards of the Army Profession, leaders are now seen as inhibiting their ability to develop the future of the profession and socialize the next generation of Soldiers and leaders. Both of these potential threats, the erosion of trust, and the corrosion of professional identity, are by themselves significant challenges. However, set in the context of the uncertain and complex environment of the 21st century, they could result in significant damage to overall military readiness (Military Review Journal, 2013).

Leaders are trusted only to the degree that people believe in their ability, consistency, integrity, and commitment to deliver. It must be earned and it takes time. Trust can't be built overnight. It requires time, effort and character. Trust is a positive expectation that another will not—through words, actions, or decisions—act opportunistically (Boon and Holmes, 1991). It is also a history-dependent process based on relevant but limited samples of experience (Rotter, 1980). In the less chaotic environment, where family and friends exist, trust is regarded as a relatively robust phenomenon. In the larger context of the organization, where supervisor and employee exist, trust is much more vulnerable. In a chaotic environment of the organization, where the unknown, or unfamiliar is met with suspicion until it has been proven reliable, the lack of trust can quickly become the overarching attitude. This lack of trust is not to be considered unreasonable, but a natural strategy for survival. Without trust, any type of relationship is destined for failure.

## The Problem Statement

As the Department of Defense again embarks on a program to transform the armed forces to address future threats, leadership, based on high levels of trust, will facilitate the successful implementation of this program. Like the other services, the U.S. Army will need to promote transformational leadership to recruit, train, and retain military personnel with the skills, knowledge, imagination, judgment, and motivation to pursue dynamic change in the 21st century.

The concept of trust is critical to leadership. DOD recognizes that the retention of committed personnel and creating a climate of innovation are important components of its transformation strategy. Trust in organizational leadership has been linked to organizational commitment and turnover intent (Dirks & Ferrin, 2002; Milligan, 2003; Vadell, 2008). Given that these findings support the transformational goals set forth in the 2014 QDR, there is a need to examine the relationship of trust in leadership on officer commitment and retention.

The problem in this research is the perceived lack of trust that officers have in their leadership. Specifically, the perceived lack of trust that captains hold with their leadership and how this perceived lack of trust may be directly connected to an *intent to leave* the U.S. Army. Previous research suggests that the lack of *trust* and *commitment* impact an employee's decision to remain with an organization, (Milligan, 2003). Trust in leadership is among the most prevalent reasons why an individual chooses to leave the Air Force, (Vadell, 2008). This study helps illuminate how *trust* in leadership is a similar problem within the U.S. Army, specifically with U.S. Army captains. The results of this research helps close the knowledge gap in trust by offering insight gained through this research. The gap in literature is bridged in light of the findings in this research, specifically with the addition of leadership counseling within military organizations.

The constructive power of counseling cannot be overstated. Army Regulation (AR) 600-20, page 14 states: "Commanders will ensure that all members of their command receive timely performance counseling. Effective performance counseling of officer, noncommissioned officer, enlisted soldiers, and Department of the Army civilian employees helps to ensure that they are prepared to efficiently carry out their duties and accomplish the mission. Providing regular and effective performance to all soldiers, not just those whose performance fails to meet unit standards, is a command function." This cannot be overstated in terms of importance, not only from an individual perspective but to the organization in its entirety.

Several research studies have shown that trust in leadership is one of the most important reasons why individuals tend to leave the military. As U.S. Army officials prepare several programs to transform the military to address future threats, goals and visions, trust in leadership (and effective counseling) will address the successful implementation of these programs and critically important, their successful way ahead.

The foundation of this research utilizes Milligan's leadership theory which states that trust is related to predictability, confidence, reliance, dependency, risk and vulnerability. Results of this research were measured against her findings as it relates to captains leaving the Army. Maslow's hierarchy of needs is also utilized in this research as a baseline of human needs system. Maslow's approach to education and learning looks at the entire physical, emotional, social, and intellectual qualities of an individual and how they impact on learning.

Figure two, below, is a graphic representation which portrays the knowledge gap in trust between captains and senior leaders. Addressing the narrowly defined knowledge gap in trust between expectations and actions, we have the commander. He is responsible for giving direction and facing the specific task of creating robust plans. The captain is responsible for taking action, subsequently, facing the specific problem of achieving the results envisioned by the commander. The senior leaders expected end-state, matched with what is actually produced by the subordinate, form the space within the knowledge gap. This gap is created from a combination of a lack of understanding, lack of clear guidance, lack of stated task, purpose and overall trust in counseling and communication between the senior leader and captain.

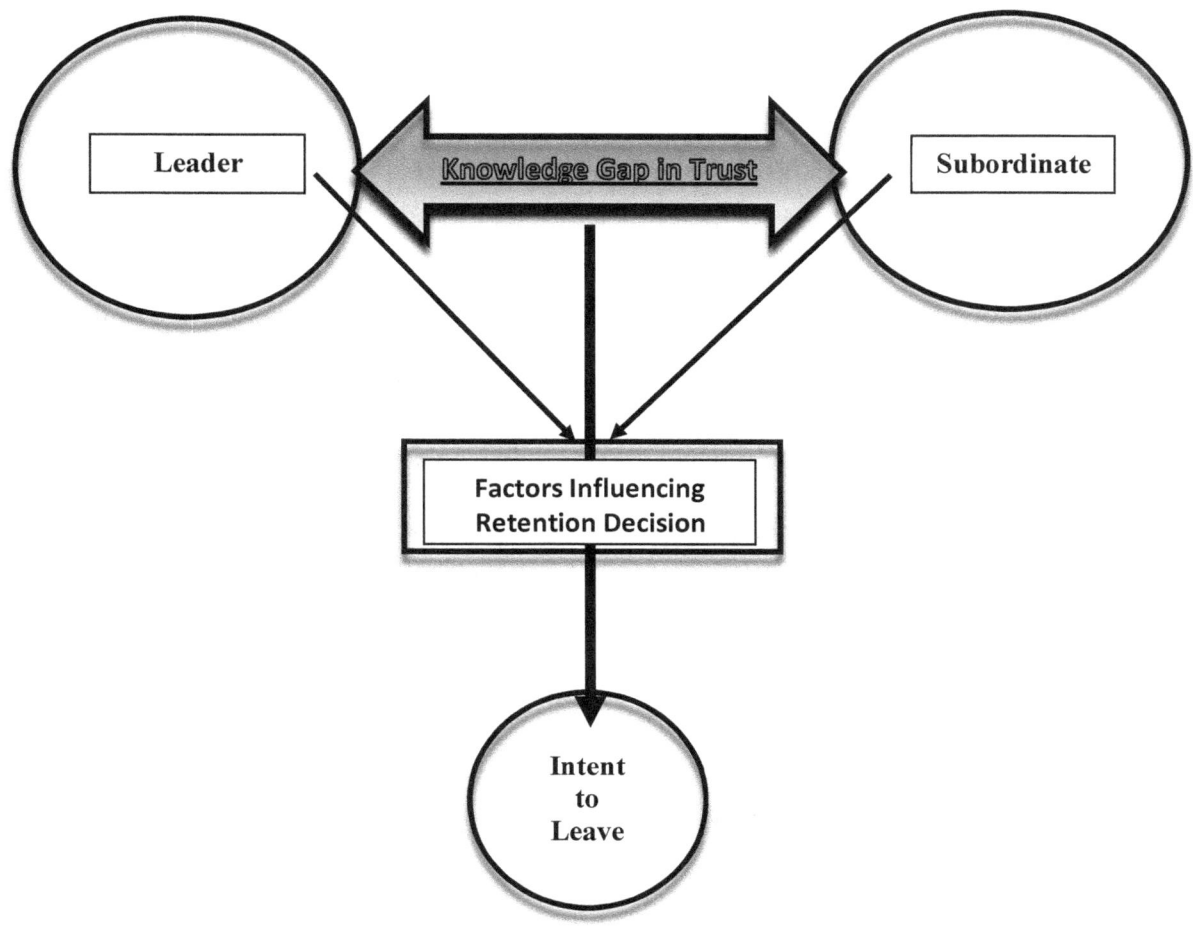

**The Knowledge Gap**

**Figure 2**

<u>Purpose of the Study</u>

The overall goal of this study was to determine a relationship between trust, commitment, and leader actions with intent to leave the military. In relation to officers leaving the military, this study looked to uncover qualities considered paramount in retaining officers after their initial commitment. A 2001 survey of officers from the Fort Leavenworth, Command and General Staff College revealed a serious lack of trust in senior leadership. The survey of 760 Army officers revealed an overall consensus of "senior leaders will throw subordinates under the bus to save their own careers."

A survey of West Point graduates shows that the military is increasingly creating a command structure that rewards conformism and ignores merit. As a result, it's losing its praised ability to cultivate entrepreneurs in uniform. Military leaders know they face a paradox. A widely circulated 2010 report from the Strategic Studies Institute of the Army War College said: "Since the late 1980s … prospects for the Officer Corps' future have been darkened by … plummeting company-grade officer retention rates."

Prior research suggested that in non-military organizations, trust in the organization impacts commitment and intentions to remain or leave the organization (Parra, 1998). This study used a survey methodology and explored possible relationships among the Independent Variables (trust, commitment, and leader actions) and the Dependent Variable (intent to leave). Using previously validated instruments to measure organizational trust, organizational commitment, leader actions with intent to leave, this research makes a determination that trust and commitment impact officer retention in the U.S Army. The sample population is among officers who have vested a minimum four years of active duty. Three survey instruments are used to meet the objective of the study.

The Knowledge Gap

The gap in trust surfaces when there is a lack of credibility with senior leadership as a result of diminished levels of trust from captains. The combination of senior leadership losing confidence in officers (captains) and the growing doubts about the trustworthiness of senior military leadership create this knowledge gap in trust between senior leaders and captains. In previous studies, this gap was also acknowledged but there were no attempts at bridging or closing the gap stemming from the research. Previous studies (Milligan 2003; Vadell 2008) articulated that trust and commitment were significant contributors to a knowledge gap, but again, no attempts at bridging this gap were documented or offered. Previous research suggested that the lack of trust and commitment may impact the decision to remain with an organization or to exit the military. This study expands on closing the knowledge gap as results of this study aid in the understanding that trust in leadership is a problem within the U.S. Army, from a captain's perspective and offers a way ahead in closing the gap through counseling techniques which is also specifically laid out in published Army Regulations.

Significance of the Study

Monumental U.S. Army structural changes, known as *Transformation*, occurred shortly after Milligan (2003) was published. As (Rost, 1993) alluded to, "Leadership is going to be much more collaborative in the new millennium, so leadership development programs must teach leaders how to think and be collaborative in leadership relationships." This observation highlights the importance of the construct of trust and the role it plays in effective leadership practices, even more so after *transformation*. As leadership becomes less about control and more about collaboration, the importance of developing and maintaining trust-based relationships increases, (Milligan, 2003). Vadell (2008) found similar results within a similar Air Force organization. The significance of this study measured levels of trust and if it is a similar issue within the U.S. Army, most notably, after Army *Transformation.*

The literature communicates the benefits of high trust environments including increased teamwork, reduced conflict, improved performance, increased leader effectiveness; all important issues to the successful implementation of the Department of Defense's 2014 QDR leader transformation strategy.

The United States remains committed to protecting its interests, sustaining U.S. leadership, and preserving global stability, security, and peace. Recognizing current fiscal realities, the Department has made a number of decisions to ensure the force remains balanced over time, even as it must begin getting smaller given fiscal constraints. We will prepare the Department of Defense for the future and preserve the health of the All-Volunteer Force as we implement reforms.

Given the importance of trust in leadership to positive organizational outcomes, the significance of this research is threefold. First, it is an empirical look into current levels of organizational trust among Army officers. Are levels of trust higher or lower than in the Air Force levels? Do Army captains exhibit the same level of trust in senior leadership as implied by the Army Command and General Staff College study or Tangredi's (2001) essay on trust in the U.S. Navy?

First, this research goes beyond subjective reports on the lack of trust in senior leadership and attempts to systematically measure trust in leadership using Sashkin's MBCA. Secondly, this research examined one facet of leadership and its impact on commitment and an intent to leave the Army. Retention is paramount to military readiness. With a considerable amount of time and resources expended every year to retain military personnel, and with evidence provided by the Army Command and General Staff College and the Army War College, dissatisfaction with leadership is an increasing factor in junior officers' decision to leave military service, an examination into what it is about leadership that is impacting these decisions is relevant and could lead to recommendations for improving leadership.

The last issue of significance is the potential outcomes from the knowledge gained by this research. Leading in a manner that creates and nurtures trusting relationships and makes trust a central principle in the Army culture may have rewards in the attraction and retention of young officers in military service. Assessing trust in Army culture may provide additional knowledge into the relationship between trust and retention and trust and commitment and lead to ways to improve Army leadership through training and leadership development efforts and to meet the needs of its current workforce and the demands of the future.

The following research questions guide this study:

Research Questions

1. What is the relationship between organizational trust with intent to leave the Army?

2. What is the relationship between organizational commitment with intent to leave the Army?

3. What is the relationship between leader actions with intent to leave?

CHAPTER 2.  LITERATURE REVIEW

Introduction

Army Leadership Doctrine: In the early 1800's, the Prussian Army (Prussia consisted of nearly the entirety of Europe with Berlin as its capital) developed an operating model called the Auftragstaktik or "mission-oriented tactics" which enabled it to consistently overcome knowledge gaps. The main idea of *Auftragstaktik* is that "commanders give subordinate officers general directions of *what* is to be done, allowing them freedom to determine *how* to do it" (Nielsen 1987). The first step was to change its culture by creating a meritocratic officer corps which valued independent thinking and initiative. The German Army has practiced *Auftragstaktik* for over 200 years, originating back to the Prussians' need to reinvent their military doctrine after their defeat at Jena by Napoleon in 1806.

The leader who turned the culture into a system was Helmuth von Moltke, who fostered high levels of autonomy and worked out how to simultaneously achieve subordinate alignment. His answer to the gap in trust between leader and subordinate officer was to limit direction to defining and expressing the essential intent; he closed the gap by allowing each level to define what it would achieve to realize the intent; and he dealt with the effects gap by giving individuals freedom to adjust their actions in line with intent. The result was to make strategy and execution a distinction without a difference. The organization no longer simply plans and implements but goes through a "thinking–doing cycle" of learning and adapting. Such a model will only work if people are competent and share basic values and most of all trust. Von Moltke invested considerable time and resources in developing junior officers, an activity which aided in grooming officers for the future Army.

The principles of Auftragstaktik have since been adopted by armed forces across the world, particularly those of the North Atlantic Treaty Organization (NATO), under the name "mission command." The model is scalable and transferable, and it is robust because it is not a new idea but a set of practices which evolved over a long period. The theory behind it stands in contrast to the scientific and engineering approaches which dominated management thinking until the 1980s.

As esoteric as it may appear, the concept expressed by the term *Auftragstaktik* is now rooted in U.S. military doctrine. After a first adoption of mission-orders in 1986 in the Field Manual (FM) 100-5, *Operations*, *Auftragstaktik* has become one of the central concepts of the U.S. Army, specifically with the publishing of the 2011 Army Doctrine Publication (ADP) 3-0, Unified Land Operations and the yearly publishing of the QDR.

QDR 2014, like its predecessor, is intended to be a strategy-driven, four-year assessment that balances the preparations of the present with the anticipated challenges of the future. Obviously, the first step in developing any strategy is the identification of objectives and the environment in which those objectives are to be pursued. In fact, the QDR 2014 report opened with a section that specified the assumptions about the future security environment that were used in guiding the review, much of the content revolved around transforming the Army training techniques for the smaller fighting force of the future. By end of FY16, the Army is projected to downsize from 570,000 to 450,000 and still continue to fight multiple wars on multiple continents.

Theoretical Background

There is a vast amount of research on military leadership concerns, but few on actual statistical significance. Transactional and transformational leadership studies have all been excessively brought forward in a myriad of studies, (Allen, et al., 2007; Sauer,

2011). Research specific to trust and military retention, however, appears much less abundantly.

A major issue seen in the military of 2015 is, again the downsizing of the Army as seen before after the first Gulf War. Schlosser (2003) addressed the issue and the impact on officers who were forced to retire or leave active duty in order to achieve the mandated reduction of Army strength from 781,000 in 1991 to 480,000. Schlosser (2003) findings were 3% positive, 48% negative and 49% neutral. Similar to Gulf War Syndrome, the higher the rank and longer YOS and therefore the closer to the 1993-96 force out period of many officers, the higher the levels of negativity toward the process. The most common themes of negativity were based upon the perceptions of being overcommitted without adequate manpower, the absence of experienced non-commissioned officers and the accelerated promotion of officers before they reached adequate levels of experience. Trust in leadership was adversely impacted by the relatively common view that Army leaders were unaware of the implications of a reduced strength Army. In short, trust in leadership is not a new theme in the military, just not highly publicized.

Previous research on military leadership also attempted to describe how leadership is swayed in one direction or another based off of leaders morals. Hannah and Avolio (2010) constructed a leadership theory on the observable moral action of leaders. The extent to which a leader chooses moral action has been termed *moral potency* or *moral conation* (Hannah & Avolio, 2010; Hannah et al., 2011). Hannah and Avolio (2010) define moral potency as a "psychological state marked by an experienced sense of ownership over the moral aspects of one's environment, reinforced by efficacy beliefs in the capabilities to act to achieve moral purpose in that domain, and the courage to perform ethically in the face of adversity and persevere through challenges," (p. 292).

Trust is the foundation of transformational leadership and a prerequisite of organizational change, (Fairholm, 1994). Trust is the confidence that employees give to management and the degree to which they believe what management tells them (Sashkin, 1996). Transactional leadership is defined as the management of interactions between leaders and followers, (Sashkin, 2000).

The corporate world has similarities to the U.S military within in the realm of leadership. Matthews (2006) demonstrated how the traditional process of leadership is intellectualized into the setting of motivating and influencing the groups to accomplish certain goals for any organization, military or civilian. With an increasingly global interdependent economy, the employment of new technology, and the changes of dynamics in military leadership, the analysis of the link between trust and organizational leadership as it is expressed within the U.S. Army, becomes central to study the effectiveness of the leadership strategies within the military, Vadell (2008). Milligan (2003) assessed similar leadership practices from the Air Force, addressing real-world situations where the composition of forces were drastically changing and discovered a simultaneously increasing struggle in sustaining retention rates.

As the military of 2015 continues to downsize, officers are concerned with their future in the military while leaders are concerned with balancing the decreasing numbers with future military mission accomplishment. The conundrum: military leadership must keep its force trained and prepared; conversely, it cannot carry a large land-war Defense Department when there is no large land war. Retaining the top qualified officers is the challenge for today's shrinking military (Hagel, 2014).

Army officer's often have taken the role of a traditional leadership style, much as it was defined by Weber (1947). The effectiveness of leadership is built upon from previous leaders so that newer leaders can act upon and are perceived to have control and power because their predecessors had those essential elements. It is the position, not the leader per se, that calls for loyalty by the subordinated individual. Weber's work defines three basic leadership styles (traditional, charismatic and bureaucratic) and have produced a wide range of theoretical work in leadership that often reflects the ever-shifting emphasis of organizational operations and communications in dynamically changing industries. Rather than view leadership as merely a product of personality traits, styles, and characteristics, researchers increasingly viewed leadership as a process-oriented function along an ever-expanding continuum.

The way we see leads to what we do, and what we do leads to the results we get. So if we want to create significant change in results, we can't just change attitudes or techniques; we have to change the basic paradigms out of which they grow, Covey (1994). True leadership describes unified action by leaders and followers working together to jointly achieve mutual goals. As Kouzes and Posner, (2002) point out, "at the heart of collaboration is _trust_."

### Army _Transformation_

U.S. Army transformation is renowned for its emphasis on acquiring modern information networks and other advanced technologies, but less so for creating new force structures. The dramatic exception to this pattern is the U.S. Army transformation plan, forged in 2004, shortly after Milligan's work was published.

The plan implemented major changes on how Army forces were to be structured. The centerpiece of transformation plan for restructuring was the creation of the "modular brigade combat team" (BCT), applied to all combat brigades in the active Army. Unlike old combat brigades, which were embedded in divisions and drew upon them for essential support, the new BCTs are to be entirely self-contained with combat and support units, and deployable on their own. Accompanying these BCTs are parallel, modular-creating changes to the Army command and control structure as well as its combat support and combat service support (CS/CSS) assets, and its aviation assets. The effect is to spread the concept of modularity across virtually the entire Army force structure.

The Army force structure that existed in the pre-transformation years reflected several decades of experience that took place during World War II, the Cold War, and the post-Cold War decade of the 1990s. Coverage of this history is important as it helps illuminate the magnitude of the complex task of transformation confronting the Army. The Army that existed in 2001 reflected this historical legacy, but its burdensome structure required important changes to carry out expeditionary missions. The challenge facing the Army was to make these changes in ways acquiring the necessary capabilities, but without throwing out the baby with the bathwater, (Kugler, 2008). In layman's terms, continue to fight multiple wars with less money and manpower, while integrating newer technology to a newer fighting force.

The overall purpose of this sweeping conversion or transformation into modular forces is to make the Army more flexible, agile, and rapidly deployable for expeditionary missions and better able to carry out modern doctrines and force operations for the Information Age. Based off of this transformation of Army in its entirety, the future Army was to be quite different from the force posture that existed when transformation began. The idea was that an Army composed of 45 BCTs and armed with networked communication weapons systems and associated assets would be able both to conduct major combat operations and to perform the sustained stabilization and reconstruction missions, such as the one that have taken place in Afghanistan and Iraq through 2015.

Trust and Army transformation

Within the realm of trust and Army transformation, this literature combination is still expanding. (Shamir and Ben-Ari, 2000) suggest that a change occurred as a result of the growing complexities of assignments and requirements. In both Milligan (2003) and Vadell (2008) they viewed the increased OPTEMPO as the greatest strain on the military force and their families. These researchers suggest that military organizations are undergoing fundamental environmental transformations that require new ways of leadership that maintain unit members' internalized commitment under conditions of decreasing support from traditional authority structures. They suggest three such transformations. First, militaries are becoming more open systems. This openness is the outcome of participating in "non-military missions, pluralistic and diverse personnel, heightened role of the media and a plethora of channels of interaction between the military and wider publics." The second transformation is that to a greater extent "military leaders are faced with serious problems of credibility and legitimacy due to changes in cultural attitudes to the use of force, increased involvement in peacekeeping and peace enforcement, and participation in multicultural and multilingual frameworks". Lastly, Shamir and Ben-Ari (2000) both highlight the impact of rapid introductions of new technologies, often times from within ad hoc frameworks that create demands for adaptable military forces, conducive to the environment, new technology and leadership hurdles, in relation to overall predictability, confidence, reliance, dependency, risk and vulnerability; the ultimate premise of the current study.

Trust in leadership

Trust in leadership and trust in employees impact overall organizational commitment (Milligan, 2003). Milligan argued that trust remains an intricate and delicate construct related to predictability, confidence, reliance, dependency, risk and vulnerability. Therefore, *Trust* and *Commitment*, and *Leader Actions*, as it relates to captains intent to leave the Army, was measured against primarily Milligan's findings but also Vadell's research findings.

Vadell (2008) argued that when the subordinate leaders envision a different strategy, although still aligned with given intent than their senior leader, they can attempt to persuade senior leader to alter the strategies execution. If the senior leader does not change the vision, the subordinate leader has three possible decisions: abandon their own vision, follow the senior leaders' vision, or shirk the senior leaders' vision altogether and work an alternate agenda, becoming intentionally disconnected from his senior leader, hence, the disconnect.

The way an individual emerges as a leader is by becoming a servant first, (Vadell 2008). In the servant leadership style, the authority shifts to those who are being led so that the dynamics of power and control so important to traditional leadership styles become secondary to the need to strengthen relationships of trust within the organizational hierarchy. (Perry & Mankin, 2007). Trust in leadership as it is presented in the Air Force resemble those articulated by Greenleaf (1977) and Northouse (2004), which emphasize the mutually complementary effects of community and individual for support and leadership strength. Similarly, transformational leadership motivates followers to transcend their self-interests for a collective purpose, vision, and/or mission (Feinberg, Ostroff, & Burk 2005). Finding a universally acceptable and operational definition of trust is difficult because it is shaped as much by cultural and social

perceptions as it is by organizational realities. With this vulnerability, leaders may have a

hard time developing trust from his or her followers. Conversely, managers today may

have a difficulty trusting employees as evidenced by an increasing need for continuous

supervision and quality control activities (Andersen, 2005).

Tan and Tan (2000) suggest that employees who trust the organization in which

they work will pursue a long-term career in that organization. Knowing this, retention

rates could possibly be affected as a function of trust within the organization. In early

2013, the United States Army published its vision of the ways it would focus institutional

resources toward building its next generation of leaders in the Army Leader Development

Strategy (ALDS). In describing the "competitive learning environment" of the future in

which our leaders will face, they will face patient and adaptive enemies who use time and

complexity to their advantage. The authors directed the Army shape victory now by

developing its leaders to "learn faster, understand better, and adapt more rapidly." The

2014 Quadrennial Defense Review (QDR) the Department of Defense (DOD) calls for a

complete paradigm shift of how the Army conducts business as the force once again

transforms into a post war organizational environment.

Current State of Research

Thomas, E. Ricks, a reporter for the *Washington Post*, wrote an article contending

that there was a gap between the junior and senior leaders in the U.S. Army officer corps.

The reporter shared the details of some of the more shocking remarks made by these

students attending the Command and General Staff College, about their senior leaders,

that did not cast them in a positive light. The overriding theme was that there is no trust

in the senior leadership. After this news release, many in the officer corps began to openly ask if there was a tension between junior and senior officers in the military. These events sparked internal reflection by the Army and its leadership in 2000 by senior members of the officer corps. The United States Army War College Strategic Studies Institute even listed "Improving Junior Officer Confidence in Senior Officer Leadership" as a critical potential research topic for officers. Trust, was surfaced as a systemic issue within the military. Only a handful of peer-reviewed articles challenged the topic. It remains difficult to find a significant number of related Doctoral dissertations, even through 2015!

Current research on trust in military leadership describes how leadership is swayed in one direction or another based off of leaders morals. (Hannah and Avolio 2010) constructed a leadership theory on the observable moral action of leaders. The extent to which a leader chooses moral action has been termed *moral potency* or *moral conation* (Hannah & Avolio, 2010; Hannah et al., 2011). Hannah and Avolio define moral potency as a "psychological state marked by an experienced sense of ownership over the moral aspects of one's environment, reinforced by efficacy beliefs in the capabilities to act to achieve moral purpose in that domain, and the courage to perform ethically in the face of adversity".

In early 2013, the United States Army published its vision of the ways it would focus institutional resources toward building its next generation of leaders in the Army Leader Development Strategy (ALDS). In describing the "competitive learning environment" of the future in which our leaders will face, they will face patient and adaptive enemies who use time and complexity to their advantage. Most recently, the 2014 Quadrennial Defense Review the Department of Defense (DOD) called for a complete paradigm shift of how the Army conducts business as the force, once again, transforms into a post war organizational environment. The authors directed the Army shape victory now by developing its leaders to "learn faster, understand better, and adapt more rapidly."

As the military of 2015 continues to downsize, leaders still have to keep the force trained and the institution prepared, but conversely, it cannot carry a large land-war Defense Department when there is no large land war. Retaining the top qualified captains is the challenge for today's shrinking military (Hagel, 2014). Again, echoing the words of GEN Odierno, in his "Initial Thoughts" and "Marching Orders", he labeled *trust* as "the bedrock of our honored Profession."

Three research concepts:

In order to fully illuminate the problem faced within the military, it is vital to grasp the following concepts: *trust* in military leadership, commitment, leader actions, and the intent to leave military service.

Trust in military leadership

Reciprocal trust in any organization at any level is complex. At the macro level, trust can be described as the bond holding together the unit in order to accomplish a mission. At the micro level, it could mean the difference between an absent-minded mistake or an intentional act of malice. Leadership turnovers is in the military are frequent event occurring usually every 12 months. These leadership transitions, often times, have no upfront stated goal or outcome. In the traditional change of command ceremony, a new commander (supervisor) is appointed. The employee (Soldier) is instantly placed in a position to trust this new leader, often times based off of nothing other than the rank that the commander holds. The new leader will probably not be given a plan of action, but still expectations of their ability to gain Soldiers trust are critically high. Trust in leadership is possibly the most important ingredient in the unit cohesion mix and the success of the command climate in its entirety. The absence of trust in a military unit can have devastating consequences, leading to certain mission failure or worse, ineffective readiness of a military unit.

## Commitment

Promoting a culture where the commitment between captains and the senior leadership in the U.S. Army will not be easy unless a thorough planning process is undertaken. First, a case history of leadership styles and approaches within the U.S. Army is needed. Then, connections must be drawn between the most relevant aspects of transformational and servant leadership practices and the needs demanded by reinforcing a program of retention and recruitment in the U.S. Army. Subsequently, several measures can then be aimed at uncovering how the leadership and captains throughout the hierarchy visualize the current environment of trust and its impact upon decisions of individual officers' to leave the Army, after their commitment time expires.

Developing a commitment strategy is an intellectual activity that involves discerning facts and applying rationality as well as relating to people and generating emotional commitment. Developing a strategy around pre-existing emotional commitments is courting disaster. When leadership convince themselves that they have the capability to do something that in fact they do not, strategies fail. When companies set unrealistic goals of growing to a market leadership position in two years simply because doing so will boost the CEO's share options, shareholders money is squandered on failed acquisitions and hopeless investments. So too is true within military organizations. If goal planning and solid investment strategies are not laid out over a period time and adhered to, failure is likely to occur.

Leader Actions

Most recently the U.S. Army needed an operational definition of the term *toxic leadership* because commanders and other interested senior leaders expressed difficulty in isolating the phenomenon in a uniform manner. More than 50% of first-term Soldiers considered leaving the Army because of mistreatment by superiors. Aubrey (2013) conducted a pilot study and the result was a set of general themes that described the distinctive elements of toxic leadership in the U.S. Army. Participants identified dysfunctional command climate, employee anti-social behavior, reduced trust and commitment, abusive supervision, unethical and abusive behaviors, and permissive environment as indicative of toxicity in U.S. Army organizations. Results showed that culture, climate, and situational factors may form a toxic pyramid and have a profound influence on toxicity determination in U.S. Army leadership. Aubrey (2013) recommended that future research needs to explore the perceptions of mid-career personnel to validate and expand on the body of knowledge pertaining to trust in military leadership.

Purpose has the power to shape our lives only in direct proportion to the power of the priority we connect it to. "Purpose without priority is powerless." Papasan (2013). Leader actions are scrutinized to an infinite level in the military. What leaders say and do or fail to say or do can make all the difference in terms of how subordinates view them holistically. Leaders who trust their subordinates and have a good relationship with them can spend more time on their own development rather than continually overseeing subordinates (Mayer, Davis, & Schoorman, 1995). Crockett, Gaetner, and Dufur concurred by adding that trust is the basis for effective delegation, two-level communication, receiving feedback, and a sense of team spirit. The delegation and relinquishing of various responsibilities to subordinates improves the quality of the supervisor's job because it enables the supervisor to have higher job visibility which leads to promotional opportunities. Further, the subordinates' ability to be effective, reliable, and consistent leads to a high performance work team that helps the supervisor achieve his or her goals. This ultimately leads to higher overall job satisfaction and unit retention.

Intent to leave

Officer retention statistics, and the studies that often accompany them, offer insight into why officers elect to forego Army service. The statistics and information utilized in this study were gathered by the U.S. Army Recruiting Command and sub-elements of the Human Resources Command. These statistics are concerned only with Captains who have reached their Active Duty Service Obligation, or have reached the point in their career in which they can opt to walk away from the Army unencumbered by an obligation for education, promotion, or some other benefit. Officers reach this point after their promotion to Captain, so the attrition rate of Captains is the most inclusive statistic indicating the officer's intention to stay or leave the Army.

Prior research suggests that trust in the organization through its agents, impact commitment and intentions to leave the organization (Parra, 1998). The U.S. Army has been operating as an Effects-Based Operation for most of its recent history (Davis, 2002). EBO is a military concept that emerged during the Persian Gulf War for the planning and conduct of operations. It's a process for obtaining a desired strategic outcome or "effect" on the enemy through the synergistic and cumulative application of the full range of military and non-military capabilities at all levels of conflict.

In addition to the importance of trust in leadership, serving as a commissioned officer differs from other forms of Army leadership by the quality and breadth of expert knowledge required, in the measure of responsibility attached, and in the magnitude of the consequences of inaction or ineffectiveness. An enlisted leader swears an oath of obedience to lawful orders, while the commissioned officer promises to, "well and faithfully discharge the duties of the office." This distinction establishes a different expectation for discretionary initiative. Officers should be driven to maintain the momentum of operations, possess courage to deviate from standing orders within the commander's intent when required, and be willing to accept the responsibility and accountability for doing so. While officers depend on the counsel, technical skill, maturity, and experience of subordinates to translate their orders into action, the ultimate responsibility for mission success or failure resides with the commissioned officer in charge.

Within organizations, interpersonal trust between supervisors and subordinates has been shown to significantly influence perceptions of accurate performance appraisals (Fulk, Brief, & Barr, 1985); organizational commitment, morale, turnover, absenteeism, and cost in untapped potential (Diffie-Couch, 1984). In addition, interpersonal trust between supervisors and subordinates improves the quality of communication (Muchinsky, Yeager, 1978), citizenship behavior (McAllister, 1995), and problem solving and decision making (Hurst, 1984). Trust among leadership may also be necessary for delegation of decision making to take place (Katzenbach & Smith, 1993).

With an increasingly global interdependent economy, the employment of new technology, and the changes of dynamics in military leadership, the analysis of the link between trust and organizational commitment as it is expressed within the U.S. Army becomes central to study the effectiveness of leadership strategies in the military, Vadell (2008).

Prior research supported this argument. Specifically, Ouchi (1981) affirmed that trust between individuals involves expectations of consistent or reliable behavior. Rotter (1980) defined trust as an "expectancy held by an individual or group that the work, promise, or written statement of another individual or group can be relied upon" (p. 444). Golembiewski and McConkie expanded on the topic of trust and confidence by writing that it "implies reliance on, or confidence in, some event, process, or person" (p. 133). Gabarro defined trust in terms of consistency of behavior and posited that "judgments about trust in working relationships become specific based on accumulation of interactions, specific incidents and events".

Griffin defined trust as "the reliance upon the characteristics of an object, or the occurrence of an event, or the behavior of a person in order to achieve a desired but uncertain objective in a risky situation" (1967). Rempel, Holmes, and Zanna, found that trust develops from interpersonal relationships between supervisors and subordinates based on the mutual degree of reliability, confidence, and security (1985). McAllister suggested that the complexity and uncertainty inherent in managerial work often require trust in order to achieve coordinated action (1995). Schindler and Thomas found that trust is based on evaluations of integrity, competence, commitment to one another, consistency, and openness regardless of whether the relationship is between oneself and a supervisor, a subordinate, or a peer. "Trust is based on perceptions of prior performance." (1993).

## Change in Demographics

The demographics of the United States are changing rapidly, this change in demographics in the workplace impacts trust. The more unlike each other employees are, the more ambiguity that might exist in their relationship, (Franta, 2000). Working with people whom one perceives as dissimilar to oneself can increase apprehension and suspicion and could possible raise the level of distrust. Doney, Cannon, and Mullen emphasize that "the importance and benefits of trust, and the emerging multicultural workplace highlight the need to understand how trust develops and the ways cultural impacts the trust building process." All of these converging trends make trust a key competitive issue for organizations.

## Future of Military Leadership

In early 2014, the Army Chief of Staff, GEN Odierno, commented on the future military leaders as the Army transitions to a smaller force. He stated, "we must revitalize how we train and prepare our future leaders." The chairman, Joint Chiefs of Staff--both former and present--the joint chiefs--both former and present--and the joint staff all participated in a study by completing the Bolman and Deal Leadership Orientations Survey and the Sashkin and Morris Frames of Reference Instrument. Their results provided convincing evidence that suggests if we can understand the differences in the various types of leadership, it can contribute to greater unity within service leadership and may promote an environment conducive to seamless interoperability.

Contemporary reviews of trust and military leadership research have called attention to the importance of studying the organizational context in which leadership unfolds. Past researchers have noted the need for increasingly sophisticated studies of leadership processes within complex and challenging environments. Halpin summarized historical changes that have influenced the context of leadership within the military environment and discusses the implications of these historical events for the content of future research on military leadership (2011).

Military Leadership Doctrine

Army Field Manuals (FM) govern everything that is done or acted upon within the military. FM's are used as a baseline of thought or actions to take in any given situation. FM 6-22 describes the character attributes and core competencies required of contemporary leaders. Character is based on the attributes central to a leader's make-up, and competence comes from how character combines with knowledge, skills, and behaviors to result in leadership. Inextricably linked to the inherent qualities of the Army leader, the concept of BE-KNOW-DO represents specified elements of character, knowledge, and behavior described in FM 6-22.

FM 6-22 notes the model's basic components center on what a leader is and what a leader does. The leader's character, presence, and intellect enable the leader to master the core leader competencies through dedicated lifelong learning. The balanced application of the critical leadership requirements empowers the Army leader to build high-performing and cohesive organizations able to effectively project and support land power. An enduring expression for Army leadership is BE-KNOW-DO. Army leadership begins with what the leader must BE - the values and attributes that shape character. KNOW – what the leader must be knowledgeable of, and DO- what the leader must DO in their role of accomplishing the mission. It may be helpful to think of these as internal and defining qualities possessed all the time. As defining qualities, they make up the identity of the leader.

Unit training and leader development are critical to prepare for operations in a complex environment. Accordingly, they are the most important things a unit does. The Army must focus on three strategic ends for training the Total Force: training units to be versatile and ready to support combatant commanders worldwide; developing military and civilian leaders to meet the challenges of the 21st century; and holding commanders responsible for the development and execution of progressive, challenging and realistic training guided by the doctrine of mission command. The outcome of these efforts will be more adaptive forces capable of achieving regional alignment or mission tailoring as required. Training for operational adaptability will take place at home station and combat training centers, in Army institutions and while deployed. During this critical transition period, Army leaders must recognize that problems do not have predetermined solutions, so training and leader development must continue to foster creativity at every level, Army Strategic Planning Guidance, (2013). "Trust and respect between leaders and subordinates are paramount, Army Chief of Staff, General Odierno, (2012, Caucus conference).

Data obtained through previous command forums, site visits, and through an Army-wide job satisfaction survey demonstrate that the force is concerned that in winding down from the campaigns in Iraq and Afghanistan, the Army will establish stifling, risk-averse, zero-defect command environments instead of embracing Mission Command. Indeed, the Army-wide survey suggested that this phenomenon has already started to occur. The highly kinetic, volatile, and dispersed nature of deployed operations in many cases did not allow battlefield commanders to over-control. Rather, commanders were forced to issue guidance and allow their subordinate commanders to show adaptability and take prudent risks with the commander's intent. In this type of environment, junior officers excelled. They learned to be decisive and adaptable, and they developed mutual trust and shared understanding with those they led.

Milligan (2003) commented the military's failure to fully embrace new or modified leadership practices in order to address real-world situations where the structure of the forces was changing dramatically and the increased difficulty to sustain the military's retention rates.

Rather than move toward a proactive stance, the military is more inclined to respond reactively, focusing more on the mission rather than what needs to be revised so that followers do not lose their commitment to the mission and to the larger organizational vision – transactional leadership as initially defined by Weber (1947).

Finally, it's imperative to the lives of Soldiers as the failure of military leadership can ultimately cost countless lives. As the DOD embarked on a program to transform the Army to address future threats, transformational leadership that is based on high levels of trust will help augment the successful implementation of this program, (2014) QDR. Trust in organizational leadership has been linked to organizational commitment and turnover intent (Dirks & Ferrin, 2002) and to be the innovative process (Clegg, Unsworth, Eptiropaki & Parker, 2002). Given the goals set out in the recent Army vision of retaining high quality Officers and establishing a positive organizational climate, there is a need to examine the relationship of trust in leadership on officer retention and commitment in the Army.

## Effects Based Organizational (EBO) leadership

The military is also better known for being an effects based organization (EBO). Commanders at all levels can apply the EBO methodology to all operations. Regardless of who employs the EBO, they must think in an effects based fashion and follow the disciplined EBO methodology of predictive analysis, course of action development, planning, execution, and effects assessment, while adapting their actions and operations to changes in the environment.

Knowing that EBO is a vital part of senior military leaders school house curriculum, one can assume that rather than moving toward a proactive stance, the military's leadership is more inclined to respond with an EBO mindset, focusing more on mission accomplishment so that followers maintain commitment to the mission and to the larger organizational vision. Under EBO mindset, transformational leaders exist but are few and far between. This EBO mindset could be act as a factor of consideration for captains in deciding whether to remain on active duty or leave the military service.

With EBO leadership being applied to the lower-level needs and being more managerial in style, it is a foundation for transformational leadership which applies to higher-level needs. EBO leaders are concerned with processes rather than forward-thinking ideas. These types of leaders focus on contingent reward or contingent penalization. Contingent rewards are given when the set goals are accomplished on-time, ahead of time, or to keep subordinates working at a good pace at different times throughout completion.

## Transformational leadership

Theorist Bernard Bass' Transformational Leadership Theory hypothesizes that Transformational leadership is defined based on the impact that it has on followers.

Transformational leaders garner trust, respect, and admiration from their followers, (Bass, 1998). Researchers have found that this style of leadership has a positive effect on a group. Research evidence clearly shows that groups led by transformational leaders have higher levels of performance and satisfaction than groups led by other types of leaders, (Riggio, 2009). The reason is that transformational leaders believe that their followers can do their best, leading members of the group to feel inspired and empowered.

Transformational leaders raise the bar by appealing to higher ideals and values of followers. In doing so, they may model the values themselves and use charismatic methods to attract people to the values and to the leader. Bass' theory of leadership focuses on the role of supervision, organization, and group performance; transactional leadership is a style of leadership in which the leader promotes compliance of his/her followers through both rewards and punishments. Through the strength of their vision and personality, transformational leaders are able to inspire followers to change expectations, perceptions, and motivations to work towards common goals.

Bass' theme is that leadership is a relationship of power for a specific purpose that is consistent, or eventually consistent, with the motives, needs, and values of both the leader and the led. Leaders in some way satisfy the motives and tap into the values of their followers, whereas power-wielders are intent only on realizing their own purposes. Whether or not the people over whom they exert their power share the purposes, motives, and values is inconsequential to the power-wielder. To the leader this sense of unity and shared values is their source of transforming influence. Important to be more than wielding power or manipulating others, leadership should be seen as a moral endeavor.

Conceptual Framework

The foundation of the conceptual framework supported leadership theory of

Pamela Milligan. Milligan added a military dimension to previous theories (Bass) and

studies of leadership and pointed a way to clear up the confusion that sometimes exists as

we focus on leadership traits, roles or situations within military leadership. Milligan

helped to define the distinct nature of leadership as a separate behavior and activity to

that of management. That shift alone allowed people to view the topic in a more

philosophical way. Milligan's general theory of leadership helps us begin to understand

what it is that makes a leader different from managers and why leadership is a significant

force in society and especially in the military.

Milligan explained in detail the theory of transformational leadership It is also

vital in terms of understanding the current research. Research evidence clearly shows

that groups led by transformational leaders have higher levels of performance and

satisfaction than groups led by other types of leaders, (Riggio, 2009). Transformational

leaders believe that their followers can do their best, leading members of the group to

feel inspired and empowered. Kouzes and Posner (2002) begin to push the concept of

trust and how it is associated as the heart of leadership. Northouse (2004) defined

transformational leadership to be the process whereby an individual engages with others

and creates a connection that raises the level of motivation in both the leader and the

follower when certain conditions arise.

Using findings from Milligan's (2003) as a measuring point and findings in

Vadell's study from 2008, this study hoisted the proverbial red flag pertaining to the

degrading level of trust in senior leadership, as reported by their own officers' in the

U.S. Army. The concept of the current research studies *trust*, *commitment* and *leader actions* against an *intent to leave* an organization. Figure three, below, shows a graphical representation of the conceptual framework describing vital elements of this research.

## Conceptual Framework

Figure 3 displays the graphical representation of the Conceptual Framework which includes the research variables, (IVs, CVs, and DVs).

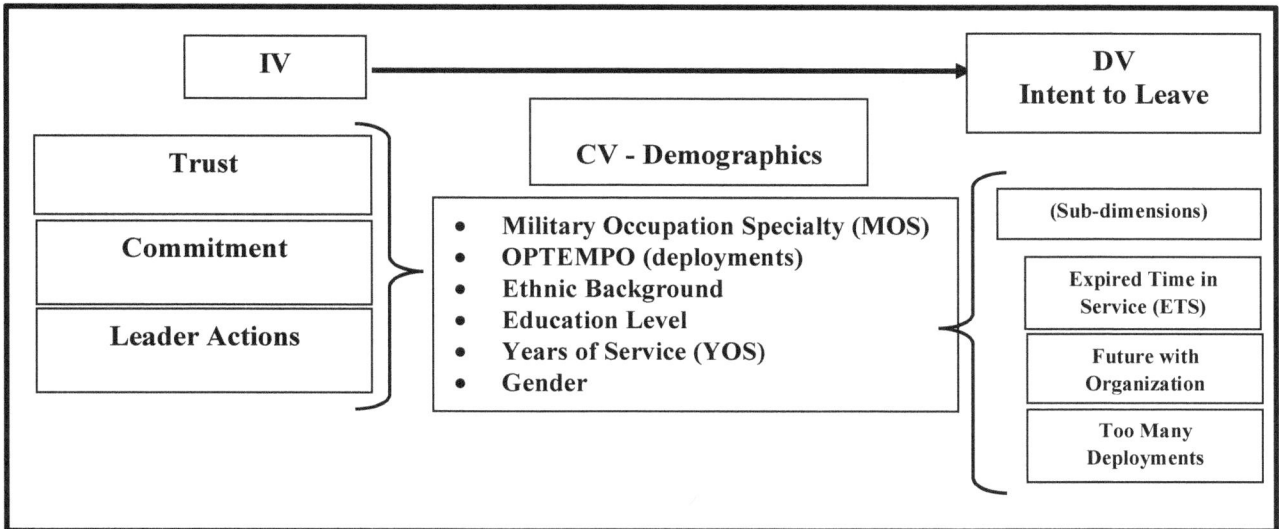

**Conceptual Framework**
**Figure 3**

## Formal Hypotheses

RQ1. What is the relationship between organizational trust with intent to leave the Army?

H1: There is a relationship between organizational trust with intent to leave the Army.

H0. There is no relationship between organizational trust with intent to leave the Army.

RQ2. What is the relationship between organizational commitment with intent to leave the Army?

H2. There is a relationship between organizational commitment and intent to leave the Army.

H0. There is no relationship between organizational commitment and intent to leave the Army.

RQ3. What is the relationship between leader actions with intent to leave the Army?

H3. There is a relationship between leader actions with intent to leave the Army.

H0. There is no relationship between leader actions with intent to leave the Army.

CHAPTER 3. METHODOLOGY

Introduction

This study used a quantitative research method in order to explore possible relationships among the established variables. Using previously validated survey instruments to measure organizational trust, organizational commitment, and leader actions, this research examined the relationship between the independent variables (IV) trust, commitment, and leader actions to determine a potential relationship with the dependent variable (DV), intent to leave the Army.

This study used a quantitative research method in order to explore possible relationships among two or more variables. To better grasp the study's methodology it's important to first measure the perceptions of trust subordinate officers' have for their leadership and to measure the factors and extent to which those perceptions of trust influence the junior officers' intention to either stay or leave military service at the traditional four-year mark. This study builds upon the findings of Milligan (2003) and Vadell (2008). Together the two sets of data and the current results form a robust baseline of data in which military leaders can utilize in their organizational growth which may influence the individual's officer's intention to remain in the service after their initial four year commitment versus having a blatant plan to exit the military.

Using previously validated surveys to measure organizational trust, organizational commitment, leader actions, and intention to leave, this research examined the relationship between these variables and whether organizational trust, as a construct, is related to organizational commitment and retention in the U.S Army.

This study incorporated a correlational design applying survey methodology previously proven effective and reliable by Milligan (2003) and Vadell (2008).

Research Method and Design

The study determined the relationships with the constructs mentioned. The goal was to explore the relationship between the independent variable and the dependent variable among the sample population of available captains attending the Captains Career Course in Fort Lee, VA. Due to mandatory concerns regarding confidentiality and anonymity, all surveys were handled by the researcher. Additionally, only captains enrolled in the Combined Arms Support Command (CASCOM) career course were surveyed. With CASCOM's granted consent and survey approval, surveys were distributed and administered per Trident University guidance. After completion, all surveys were immediately collected, accessible only to the researcher. In accordance with Trident University policy, all completed surveys remain under the control of the researcher and under lock and key in a safety lock box for a period of no less than five years. Incomplete or illegible surveys were shredded and destroyed. After the five year storage minimum time frame has passed, all surveys are shredded and destroyed. The analysis of survey data employed Statistical Package for the Social Sciences (SPSS) version 22, with finding statistical significance between variables.

Prior documented interviews with commanders at the O-5 / O-6 level focus groups revealed a perceived lack of trust and confidence in subordinate leaders' expertise (knowledge, skills, and abilities) for garrison (home station) operations. They cited a lack of experience among midgrade officers (captains) required for competence in the home station environment. "These factors reinforce the concept that competence and expertise are major components of trust at the individual and organizational level", Snider (2012).

At the organizational level, researchers categorized trust as having four components that reflect the nature of trust:

Credibility of *competence*.
*Benevolence* of motives.
*Integrity* with the sense of fairness and honesty.
*Predictability* of behavior.

These components apply not only to individuals, but also Army organizations. It is critical for organizations to have the ability to accomplish tasks and missions in an efficient, effective, and ethical manner. Also critical is the perception that organizational procedures (policies and regulations) are established for the common and greater good. Further, an essential element of trust is the feeling and belief that members behave according to a set of values that apply to all within the profession. Finally, trust builds on consistent achievement of moral objectives that advance both stakeholder and member feelings of good will. Violation of these conditions may lead to a gap in trust or, more destructively, a sense of distrust.

## Data Collection and Population Sampling

The research focused strictly on a study population of Army captains at the Fort Lee, Virginia, Captains Career Course. The minimum acceptable sample size was set at 250, maximum was 400. The optimal target population number and proposed sample size was 350. For this research a statistical significance level of .05 was selected because of the acceptance by the scientific community that something with a 95% chance of being true is good enough to be believed (Creative Research Systems, 2013). With this significance level and proposed sample size *(n* = 350) power is calculated to be .90. Where the significance level expresses the probability of rejecting the null hypothesis when it is true (Type I error), power is the probability of rejecting the null hypothesis when it is false and should be rejected (Type II error). For this research, there was a 90% probability that the null hypothesis would be appropriately rejected.

Data Collection Tools

The survey instruments were: the Management Behavior Climate Assessment (MBCA) Survey for measures of *trust* and *leader actions*; the continuance *commitment* scales survey; and the *intent to leave* survey. All three instruments were previously validated by (Levin, 1999), (Milligan, 2003) and again by (Vadell, 2008). This study considered the validity on how consistent the instrument results are for repeated measurements. The lower the variation an instrument produces in repeated measurements, the higher its reliability (Hutchison, 2005). Measures for each variable were listed under each separate instrument. All participants received a letter from the researcher explaining the study. The surveys were distributed in an open auditorium, filled out and immediately collected by the researcher. There were no incentives promised or offered in the participation of the study. All participants had a choice to participate or not to participate in this study. The completed survey data was immediately collected, coded, and entered into SPSS for analysis.

The Demographic Questionnaire

This instrument simply gathered basic fundamental data such as years of service (YOS), military occupational specialty (MOS), education level, ethnic background, gender, and number of deployments. All of which were helpful in the cross-tabulation of the data analysis portion of the research. The collected demographic information was used to access the capacity for generalizing the results of the sample to the larger captain population of the U.S. Army.

## Management Behavior Climate Survey Instrument (MBCA)

The first of the three surveys, the MBCA, developed by (Sashkin, 1996) measured *trust* and the credibility of *leader actions* of senior level managers (Levin, 1999). It contained 50 statements, 24 of which were nominal in nature and 26 of which consisted of ordinal data using a five-point Likert scale: *1= Rarely / Never, 2= Seldom, 3= Occasional, 4= Usually, 5= Always / Almost Always.* Lower scores equated to low levels of perceptions of either *Trust, Commitment.,* or *Leader Action.*

This self-administered 50-questionnaire consisted of ten scales of five items. The first set of scales measured consistency in how one acts toward different people; consistency in what one tells different people; consistency in actions over time; and, consistency in what one says over time. The second set of scales, measured the credibility of *leader-actions*. These scales assessed the degree to which leadership follows though and does what it says it is going to do. The last set of scales assessed the overall trustworthiness of leadership.

Consistent with works of Lewis and Weigert (1985), Sashkin's theory of organizational trust contained consistency, credibility and trustworthiness elements. Levin found the MBCA to be a very reliable instrument which measured two expansive areas of trust: consistency and credibility. Levin found Sashkin's measure to be reliable and valid from the use of seven independent samples, two of which were military. Previous researchers found the MBCA reliable with a Cronbach's coefficient alpha ranging from .83 to .93, (Lafferty, Milligan, and Vadell).

## Organizational Commitment Survey Instrument

The second survey instrument used the continuance commitment scales to measure organizational commitment developed and validated by Meyer and Allen

(1996). The commitment scale helped illustrate the relationship between commitment and intent to leave the Army. Continuance commitment refers to the employee's recognition of the costs associated with leaving the organization. (Mowday, 1979) reported that the correlations between organizational commitment questionnaire and the affective commitment scale were in fact significant (.80) which shows convergent validity between the two scales. This survey consisted of 24 questions, 13 of which were nominal in nature, 11 of which were ordinal. Each scale contained eight items for a total of twenty-four items. Responses to the scales were coded on a six - point Likert scale from: *1=Strongly Agree, 2= Moderately Agree, 3= Slightly Agree, 4= Slightly Disagree, 5=Moderately Disagree, 6= Strongly Disagree.*

The reported Cronbach's alpha coefficients ranged from .84 to .89 for the continuance commitment scale, (Vadell, 2008).

Intent to Leave Survey Instrument

The last instrument used in this research measured the intent of the respondent to leave military service, modified to address a study pertaining to the U.S. Army. Jaros (1997) used a measure very similar to the one used in this study, which showed a reliability alpha of .80.

The ten-question *Intent to Leave* survey measured the respondents' intention to leave the military with three sub-dimensions: "Expired Time in Service (ETS)"; "Future with the Organization"; and "Feelings of Being Deployed too Often or (OPTEMPO)". Questions one to four are rated on a five-point Likert-type scale. For questions one to four, low scores indicate high intentions to stay in the Army. Questions five to ten are rated on a four-point Likert-type scale ranging from 1 (Strongly Disagree) to 4 (Strongly Agree): "I am actively looking for another job"; "I will remain in the Army after current commitment (reverse scored)"; "I often think of leaving the Army"; "I intend to leave the Army because of Too Many Deployments"; "If another organization offered me a job now, I would leave the Army, even if the salary were equal"; and "As soon my commitment is complete, I will leave the Army". For questions five to ten, low scores indicate high intentions to leave the organization. All items except question 6 are positively-worded and require no reflection at a later stage.

## Independent Variables

The IV's for this study were Trust and Commitment, and, Leader Actions. The first of the three surveys, *the MBCA*, measured both *trust* and *leaders actions*. The second survey, *The Organization Commitment Scale Survey* used the continuance commitment scales to measure *commitment.*

## Dependent Variable

The third and final survey measured the DV, Intent to Leave. Sub-dimensions variable of the *Intent to Leave Survey* include: "Expired Time in Service (ETS)" (with questions 6 & 10); "Feelings of the Future with the Current Organization" (with questions 1-4); "Personal Importance with the Current Organization" (with questions 5 & 9); and "Feeling of Being Deployed too Often" (with questions 7 & 8). Low scores indicated high intentions to stay in the Army.

## Control Variables

The control variables included: Years of Service (YOS), coded on a scale from, *1= (1 to 4), 2= (5 to 10), 3= (11+);* Military Occupational Specialty, (MOS), coded on a scale from, *1= Combat, 2= Combat Support, 3= Sustainment;* Education Level coded on a scale from, *1 = Bachelors, 2 = Masters, 3 = PhD*; Ethnic Background, coded on a scale

from, *1 = Asian American, 2 = African American, 3 = Hispanic, 4 = Native American, 5 =*

*Caucasian;* Gender, scaled from, *1 = male, 2 = female*; Number of Deployments (Number

of Times Deployed) coded on a scale from *0 = (0), 1 = (1-3), 2 = (4+).*

<u>Statistical Analysis</u>

       Data from surveys and demographic reporting information was tabulated, coded

and entered using the SPSS software, version 22. All statistical analyses were pegged at

the 95% confidence level (p=.05) and a significance level of .05 level with a sample size

of (N=362) and power was calculated at .90. Using multiple regression and bivariate

correlation, the researcher determined if a relationship exists between intent to leave

(ITL) and *trust, commitment,* or *leader actions,* while controlling for the covariates of

YOS, MOS, education level, ethnicity, gender, and number of deployments.

Table 1

*Statistical Analysis / Variables*

| Research Question | IV / CV | DV | Statistical Method |
|---|---|---|---|
| RQ1. What is the relationship between organizational trust with intent to leave the Army? | IV – Trust CV – MOS, YOS, Ethnicity, Number of Deployments, Education level, Gender | ITL | Multiple Regression |
| RQ2. What is the relationship between organizational commitment with intent to leave the Army? | IV – Commitment CV – MOS, YOS, Ethnicity, Number of Deployments, Education level, Gender | ITL | Multiple Regression |

| RQ3. What is the relationship between leader actions with intent to leave the Army? | IV – Leader Actions CV – MOS, YOS, Ethnicity, Number of Deployments, Education level, Gender | ITL | Multiple Regression |

CHAPTER 4. DATA ANALYSIS AND PRESENTATION OF RESULTS

Introduction

This chapter presented a complete statistical analysis of the research data. The first section explained the results received from all respondents. Section two provided a complete descriptive statistic for each instrument. Further, this chapter examined the research hypotheses and the data analysis regarding the support or rejection of the hypotheses described in this study. The final section of this chapter presented the results of each research question and the regression analysis which determined predictability between study variables.

Data Screening

The research depended on the availability of the captains at the Captains Career Course for participation. An anonymous paper survey was administered in this research to a random sample size of 400 captains selected from the student population. The survey was designed for each participant to answer all questions. The final sample size of 362 participants had responded to the research survey, resulting in a 91% response rate used in this research.

The researcher evaluated the categorical values before conducting multiple regressions and performed dummy coding using zero's and ones until all the categorical variables, minus one were accounted for (Field, 2005).

Demographics of Respondents

The researcher performed dummy coding on MOS and Ethnic Background. Ethnic Background breakdown follows: Other also represents Asian American (19), Hispanic (23), and Native American (5) for a total of (59), African American (132), Caucasian (171), Dummy coding for Ethnic Background in the Table below:

Table 1A

*Dummy coding for Ethnic Background*

|  | **Other** | **Caucasian** | **African American** |
|---|---|---|---|
| Other | 0 | 0 | 0 |
| Caucasian | 1 | 0 | 0 |
| African American | 0 | 1 | 0 |

For Military Occupational Specialty (MOS), the categories were Combat, Combat Support, and Sustainment. The researcher performed dummy coding, depicted below:

|  | **Other** | **Caucasian** | **African American** |
|---|---|---|---|
| Combat | 0 | 0 | 0 |
| Combat Support | 1 | 0 | 0 |
| Sustainment | 0 | 1 | 0 |

A snapshot of all variables, Table 2, laid the foundation for presenting future data.

Table 2

*Descriptive analysis for Continuous variables*

| *Variable* | *Mean, (SD)* | *N (%)* | *95% (CI)* |
|---|---|---|---|
| *Dependent Variables* | | | |
| Expired Time in Service (ETS) | 2.79, (.812) | 362 | (2.72, 2.87) |
| Future with Organization | 1.93, (.878) | 362 | (1.84, 2.02) |
| OPTEMPO | 1.76, (.646) | 362 | (1.69, 1.82) |

| Variable | Mean (SD) | N (%) | 95% (CI) |
|---|---|---|---|
| *Independent Variables* | | | |
| Trust | 2.46 (.285) | 362 | (2.06, 3.37) |
| Commitment | 2.80 (.129) | 362 | (2.63, 2.97) |
| Leader Actions | 3.01 (.207) | 362 | (2.07, 3.09) |
| | | | |
| *Covariates* | | | |
| Years of Service (YOS) | | | |
| 1 - 4　yrs | 6.72 (47.7) | | |
| 5 - 10　yrs | 2.21 (33.5) | | |
| 11 +　yrs | 1.07 (18.8) | | |
| | | | |
| Education | | | |
| Baccalaureate | 187 (51.7) | | |
| Masters | 165 (45.6) | | |
| Ph.D. | 10 (2.7) | | |
| | | | |
| Number of Deployments (OPTEMPO) | | | |
| 0 | 7 (1.9) | | |
| 1-3 | 260 (71.8) | | |
| 4+ | 95 (26.2) | | |

Table 3

*Descriptive analysis for Categorical Variables*

The frequency and percent are reflected below for the categorical variables: Gender, Ethnicity, and MOS.

*Table 3*

| Variable | Frequency | Percent (%) | |
|---|---|---|---|
| Gender | | | |
| Male | 275 | (76) | |
| Female | 87 | (24) | |
| | | | |
| Ethnicity | | | |
| White / Caucasian | 171 | (47.2) | |

|      | African American | 132 | (36.5) |
|------|------------------|-----|--------|
|      | Other            | 59  | (16.3) |
| MOS  |                  |     |        |
|      | Combat           | 84  | (23.2) |
|      | Combat Support   | 73  | (20.2) |
|      | Sustainment      | 205 | (56.6) |

The DV is *Intent to leave*. The three Sub-Dimensional Variables (SDV) of the *Intent to Leave* include: "ETS" (M=2.79, SD=.812); "Future with the Current Organization" (M = 1.93, SD = .878); "OPTEMPO" (M = 1.76, SD = .646). All contain measuring criteria rated on a four-point Likert-type scale, ranging from 1 "strongly disagree" to 4 "strongly agree". Low scores indicate high intentions to stay in the Army. Table 4 breaks down each of the three SDVs:

Table 4

*Descriptive Analysis for the three Dependent Variables:*

| Dependent Variable | N | Min | Max | Mean, (SD) | 95% (CI) |
|--------------------|-----|-----|-----|-------------|----------------|
| SDV1- ETS | 362 | 1 | 4 | 2.79, (.812) | (2.72, 2.87) |
| SDV2- Future with Organization | 362 | 1 | 4 | 1.93, (.878) | (1.84, 2.02) |
| SDV3- OPTEMPO | 362 | 1 | 4 | 1.76, (.646) | (1.69, 1.82) |

Descriptive Analysis for the three Independent Variables: Trust, Commitment, and Leader Actions: The Independent Variables are *Trust*, (M = 3.71, SD = .113); *Commitment*, (M = 2.80, SD = .169); and *Leader Actions*, (M = 3.76, SD = .107). *Trust* and *Leader Actions* (MBCA Survey) contained 50 questions used a five-point Likert scale: *1= Rarely / Never, 2= Seldom, 3= Occasional, 4= Usually, 5= Almost Always.*

_Commitment_ scale contained 24 questions and seven measurement criteria measured on a six - point Likert scale from: _1=Strongly Agree, 2= Moderately Disagree, 3= Slightly Agree, 4= Slightly Disagree, 5=Moderately Agree, 6= Strongly Disagree._ Table 5 displays the Descriptive Analysis for three Independent Variables.

Table 5

_Descriptive Analysis for the Independent Variables (IVs)_

| Independent Variable | N | Min | Max | Mean, (SD) | 95% (CI) |
|---|---|---|---|---|---|
| IV1- Trust | 362 | 1 | 5 | 3.71, (.113) | (2.97, 2.60) |
| IV2- Commitment | 362 | 1 | 6 | 2.80, (.169) | (2.63, 2.97) |
| IV3- Leader Actions | 362 | 1 | 5 | 3.01, (.107) | (1.17, 3.09) |

There were a total of 362 participants. Males: frequency = 275, percent = 76%; Females: frequency = 87, percent = 24%. Expired Time in Service for males were (M = 2.81, SD = .806, 95% CI [2.72, 2.91]; Females were (M = 2.72, SD = .831, 95% CI [2.55, 2.90]. According to the Army Demographics Active Duty Personnel Master File (2015), Males comprise 85.1% of the active duty members and females the remaining 14.9%. This demographic of this study is slightly different with a higher percentage of females within the population. Shown in Table 6 is the overall descriptive analysis by variable according to Gender.

Table 6

_Descriptive Analysis for Dependent Variables by Gender_

| Dependent Variable | N | Min | Max | Mean, (SD) | 95% (CI) |
|---|---|---|---|---|---|
| ETS | | | | | |
| Males | 275 | 1 | 4 | 2.81, (.806) | (2.72, 2.91) |
| Females | 87 | 1 | 4 | 2.72, (.831) | (2.55, 2.90) |

Future with Organization

| | N | Min | Max | Mean, (SD) | 95% (CI) |
|---|---|---|---|---|---|
| Males | 275 | 1 | 4 | 1.90, (.869) | (1.79, 2.00) |
| Females | 87 | 1 | 4 | 2.02, (.902) | (1.83, 2.22) |

OPTEMPO

| | N | Min | Max | Mean, (SD) | 95% (CI) |
|---|---|---|---|---|---|
| Males | 275 | 1 | 4 | 1.73, (.628) | (1.66, 1.81) |
| Females | 87 | 1 | 4 | 1.84, (.697) | (1.66, 1.99) |

Prior to running descriptive analysis on ethnicity, the researcher grouped the variables into three categories: 1 = Caucasians accounted for the highest ethnic background; frequency = 171, percent = 47.2%, followed by 2 = African American; frequency = 132, percent = 36.5%. 3 = Other; frequency = 59, percent = 16.3%. In comparison to the 2014 Army demographical data on ethnicity: Caucasians account for 57% of the active duty members and African Americans constitute 37%. The Caucasian percentage falls in this study by 10% while African Americans showed an increase by .01%. The descriptive analysis is described in Table 7 below, by ethnicity for each dependent variable.

Table 7, *Descriptive Analysis for Dependent Variables by Ethnicity*

| ETHNICITY | N | Min | Max | Mean, (SD) | 95% (CI) |
|---|---|---|---|---|---|
| ETS | | | | | |
| Other | 59 | 1 | 3 | 2.48, (.846) | (2.11, 2.84) |
| Caucasian | 171 | 1 | 3 | 2.77, (.811) | (2.72, 2.91) |
| African American | 132 | 1 | 3 | 2.80, (.072) | (2.65, 2.94) |
| Future with Organization | | | | | |
| Other | 59 | 1 | 3 | 2.26, (.253) | (1.74, 2.79) |
| Caucasian | 171 | 1 | 3 | 2.81, (.816) | (2.72, 2.91) |
| African American | 132 | 1 | 3 | 2.72, (.831) | (2.55, 2.90) |
| OPTEMPO | | | | | |
| Other | 59 | 1 | 3 | 2.00, (.745) | (1.64, 2.36) |
| Caucasian | 171 | 1 | 3 | 2.81, (.806) | (2.72, 2.91) |

| African American | 132 | 1 | 3 | 1.73, (.564) | (1.64, 1.83) |

Students in the "1-4" category accounted for the largest portion of the population: frequency = 164, percent = 45.3% with the "5-10" category: frequency = 116, percent =32%. The lowest frequency of students equate to those that have been in the Army the longest. More information is referenced in the Descriptive Analysis, Table 8 below.

Table 8

*Descriptive Analysis for the Dependent Variables by Years of Service (YOS)*

| YEARS of SERVICE | N | Min | Max | Mean, (SD) | 95% (CI) |
|---|---|---|---|---|---|
| ETS | | | | | |
| 1-4 | 164 | 1 | 4 | 2.83, (7.80) | (2.71, 2.95) |
| 5-10 | 116 | 1 | 4 | 2.72, (.788) | (2.57, 2.86) |
| 11+ | 82 | 1 | 4 | 2.82, (.918) | (2.62, 3.02) |
| Future with Organization | | | | | |
| 1-4 | 164 | 1 | 4 | 1.91, (.253) | (1.74, 2.79) |
| 5-10 | 116 | 1 | 4 | 1.96, (.859) | (1.80, 2.11) |
| 11+ | 82 | 1 | 4 | 1.91, (.878) | (1.85, 2.00) |
| OPTEMPO | | | | | |
| 1-4 | 164 | 1 | 4 | 2.00, (.745) | (1.64, 2.36) |
| 5-10 | 116 | 1 | 4 | 2.77, (.805) | (2.72, 2.91) |
| 11+ | 82 | 1 | 4 | 1.72, (.634) | (1.58, 1.86) |

Students possessing a baccalaureate degree accounted for the most commonly held degree: frequency = 201, percent = 56% followed by a Master's degree: frequency = 152, percent = 42%. The least held degree was the Ph.D.: frequency = 9, percent = .02%. According to the FY14 Army profile, the breakdown of percentage of education obtained by Captain's is Baccalaureate- 74%, Master's 21%, and Ph.D., .05%. This student population far exceeds the educational statistics of the 2014 Army with the Master's degree at nearly double the percentage for the previous year. Additional information on education is in the descriptive analysis, Table 9.

Table 9

*Descriptive Analysis for the Dependent Variables by Education*

| EDUCATION | N | Min | Max | Mean, (SD) | 95% (CI) |
|---|---|---|---|---|---|
| ETS | | | | | |
| Baccalaureates | 201 | 1 | 3 | 2.72, (7.89) | (2.61, 2.83) |
| Masters | 152 | 1 | 3 | 2.89, (.826) | (2.76, 3.02) |
| Ph.D. | 9 | 1 | 3 | 2.67, (.918) | (1.90, 3.04) |
| | | | | | |
| Future with Organization | | | | | |
| Baccalaureates | 201 | 1 | 3 | 2.04, (.838) | (1.93, 2.16) |
| Masters | 152 | 1 | 3 | 1.78, (.900) | (1.63, 1.92) |
| Ph.D. | 9 | 1 | 3 | 1.89, (.878) | (1.08, 2.70) |
| | | | | | |
| OPTEMPO | | | | | |
| Baccalaureates | 201 | 1 | 3 | 1.79, (.556) | (1.71, 1.86) |
| Masters | 152 | 1 | 3 | 1.69, (.730) | (1.57, 1.81) |
| Ph.D. | 9 | 1 | 3 | 2.22, (.833) | (1.58, 2.86) |

In regards to the survey, there was only question pertaining to MOS. Prior to generating the descriptive analysis on MOS, the researcher grouped the variables into three categories: Combat Support, Sustainment, and Combat. Sustainment accounts for the majority of the respondents at frequency = 205, percentage = 57% and Combat Support at frequency = 73, percent = 21% which is in close proximity of the Army's support ratio of 3:1 where a direct combat Soldier requires three support Soldiers for a successful operation.(McGrath, 2007). Additional MOS-related information is in Table 10.

Table 10

*Descriptive Analysis for the Dependent Variables by MOS*

| MOS | N | Min | Max | Mean, (SD) | 95% (CI) |
|---|---|---|---|---|---|
| ETS | | | | | |
| Combat Support | 73 | 1 | 3 | 2.66, (.837) | (2.46, 2.85) |
| Sustainment | 205 | 1 | 3 | 2.82, (.827) | (2.71, 2.94) |
| Combat | 84 | 1 | 3 | 2.82, (.747) | (2.66, 2.98) |
| | | | | | |
| Future with Organization | | | | | |
| Combat Support | 73 | 1 | 3 | 1.93, (.885) | (1.80, 2.18) |
| Sustainment | 205 | 1 | 3 | 1.90, (.863) | (1.78, 2.02) |
| Combat | 84 | 1 | 3 | 1.99, (.885) | (1.80, 2.18) |
| | | | | | |
| OPTEMPO | | | | | |
| Combat Support | 73 | 1 | 3 | 1.70, (.720) | (1.53, 1.87) |
| Sustainment | 205 | 1 | 3 | 1.79, (.596) | (1.70, 1.87) |
| Combat | 84 | 1 | 3 | 1.74, (.696) | (1.59, 1.89) |

Quantitative Analysis for the Research Questions

**Quantitative Analysis of Research Question 1**

The MBCA survey contained 50 questions used to measure trustworthiness that people hold with their organizational leaders. The research conducted included bivariate and multivariate statistics on the following research question:

RQ1. What is the relationship between organizational *trust* with intent to leave?

**Bivariate Statistics**

The researcher conducted bivariate analysis using Pearson correlation of the three dependent variables: Expired Time in Service (ETS), Future with Organization, Too Many Deployments (OPTEMPO), with the independent variable of *Trust*. Prior to conducting bivariate analysis, the researcher examined the data for outliers, and removed them.

**Bivariate Correlations between three Dependent Variables with Trust**

ETS has a strong negative correlation at the .01 level with Future with

Organization, (M = 2.74, SD = .848) according to the 362 students and participating in

the survey. Future with Organization (M = 1.77, SD = .918) was clearly more significant

predictor than OPTEMPO (M = 1.76, SD = .646) in relation to Trust, as reported by the

students participating in the survey. Trust (M = 2.22, SD = .733) was a significant

predictor to the level of Future with Organization. Table 11 shows the significance

between the three dependent variables with the independent variable, *Trust*.

Table 11

*Bivariate Correlations between three Dependent Variables with Trust using Pearson*

|  | 1 | 2 | 3 | 4 |
|---|---|---|---|---|
| 1. ETS | 1 | **-.248\*\*** | -090 | .084 |
| 2. Future with Organization |  | 1 | **.288\*\*** | **.279\*\*** |
| 3. OPTEMPO |  |  | 1 | -.050 |
| 4. Trust |  |  |  | 1 |

*Bold\*\* = significance p<.01*

**Assumption Checking**

To avoid violations when running hierarchical multiple linear regression, the

researcher checked the following assumptions before running the regression analysis:

normality, multi-collinearity homoscedasticity (Field, 2009). The researcher checked

each assumption with pairwise deletion for compliance. **Normality**: The researcher

checked the histogram for a bell shaped curve and p-plot for a 45-degree angle.

Normality was clear by this examination.

**Homoscedasticity**: Homoscedasticity appeared after examining the scatterplots.

The assumptions for hierarchical multiple linear regressions were checked. The Durbin-

Watson test indicated a value of 1.800. According to Field (2009), values less than 1 or greater than 3 are cause for concern (2005). **Collinearity** according to Fields exists when there is a strong correlation between two or more predictor variables (2009) and in the case of the three independent variables; the VIF values of 1.000, 1.007, and 1.035 cause no need for concern (Field, 2009).

*Multivariate Analysis*

Multiple regression analysis tested the relationship between *Trust, Commitment,* and *Leader Actions* with *Intent to Leave.* Further, the researcher determined whether or not *Trust, Commitment,* and *Leader Actions* significantly predicted an *Intention to Leave* the military. For this section, the researcher performed multiple regressions on the three dependent variables focusing on the independent variable of *Trust.*

*Results of multiple regression of DV's with IV Trust*

Hierarchical multiple regression analysis was performed. Results of the regression analysis provided confirmation for the research hypothesis. Beta coefficients for *trust* was, $\beta = .019, t = 2.083, p = .008$. The regression further revealed gender, ethnic background, and education had a negative effect on ETS when *trust* is in the model. The research indicated that *trust* was a statistically significant predictor to *Intent to Leave,* **p=.008**. For model M1, the adjusted $R2$ is -.009. This model can explain .09% variance. In model M2, when *trust* is in the model, adjusted $R2$ increases by 10% to .019. This model can explain .1.9% variance.

Table 12
*Coefficient Table for ETS with Trust*

|  |  | Unstandardized Coefficients | | Standardized Coefficients | | |
|---|---|---|---|---|---|---|
|  |  | B | Std. Error | Beta | t | Sig. |
| M1 |  |  |  |  |  |  |
|  | (Constant) | 2.681 | .257 |  | 2.445 | .000 |
|  | Caucasian | .011 | .031 | .020 | .339 | .000 |
|  | African American | .007 | .030 | .011 | .112 | .002 |
|  | Other Ethnicity | .001 | .010 | .001 | .102 | .001 |
|  | Education Level | .137 | .082 | .088 | 1.670 | .735 |
|  | YOS | .055 | .070 | .050 | .797 | .096 |
|  | MOS | .052 | .054 | .051 | .959 | .426 |
|  | Gender | -.065 | .105 | -.033 | -.618 | .338 |
| M2 |  |  |  |  |  |  |
|  | (Constant) | 2.425 | .284 |  | 8.551 | .000 |
|  | Caucasian | .011 | .031 | .020 | .339 | .000 |
|  | African American | .007 | .030 | .011 | .112 | .002 |
|  | Other Ethnicity | -.001 | -.010 | .001 | .102 | .001 |
|  | Education Level | -.133 | .082 | .086 | 1.625 | .105 |
|  | YOS | .057 | .069 | .051 | .816 | .415 |
|  | MOS | .056 | .054 | .055 | 1.034 | .302 |
|  | Gender | -.069 | .105 | -.035 | -.656 | .512 |
|  | **TRUST** | **.126** | **.061** | **.019** | **2.083** | **.008** |

a. Dependent Variable: Expired Time in Service (ETS)

Hierarchical multiple regression analysis was performed. Results of the regression analysis provided confirmation for the research hypothesis. Beta coefficients for trust was, $\beta = .041$, $t = .214$, $p = .001$. The research indicated that *Trust* was a statistically **significant predictor to Intent to Leave (p=.001).** For model 1, the adjusted $R2$ is .011. In model 2, when *Trust* is in the model, adjusted $R2$ increases by .030. This model can explain 4.1% variance, see below, Table 13.

Table 13

*Coefficient Table for Future with Organization with Trust*

| | | Unstandardized Coefficients | | Standardized Coefficients | | |
|---|---|---|---|---|---|---|
| | | B | Std. Error | Beta | t | Sig. |
| M1 | (Constant) | 1.628 | .197 | | 8.264 | .000 |
| | Caucasian | .005 | .024 | .013 | .218 | .828 |
| | African American | .007 | .030 | .011 | .112 | .002 |
| | Other Ethnicity | .003 | .010 | .001 | .102 | .001 |
| | Education Level | -.004 | .063 | -.003 | -.064 | .949 |
| | YOS | .023 | .053 | .027 | .428 | .669 |
| | MOS | .025 | .042 | .033 | .609 | .543 |
| | Gender | .097 | .081 | .064 | 1.201 | .230 |
| M2 | (Constant) | 1.694 | .219 | | 7.743 | .000 |
| | Caucasian | .004 | .021 | .013 | .217 | .826 |
| | African American | .007 | .030 | .011 | .112 | .002 |
| | Other Ethnicity | .001 | .010 | .001 | .102 | .001 |
| | Education Level | -.003 | .063 | -.003 | -.047 | .963 |
| | YOS | .023 | .053 | .027 | .423 | .673 |
| | MOS | .024 | .042 | .031 | .584 | .560 |
| | Gender | .098 | .081 | .065 | 1.212 | .226 |
| | **TRUST** | **.014** | **.066** | **.041** | **.214** | **.001** |

Dependent Variable: Future with Organization

Hierarchical multiple regression analysis was performed. Results of the regression analysis provided confirmation for the research hypothesis. Beta coefficients for trust was, $\beta = -.011$, $t = -.258$, $p = .007$. The regression further provided that MOS and Education both had negative effects on *OPTEMPO* when trust is in the model. The researcher saw that **trust was a statistically significant predictor to Intent to Leave,**

**(p= -.007).** For model 1, the adjusted $R2$ is .001. In model 2, when trust is in the model, adjusted $R2$ increases 10% to .011. This model can explain 1.1% of the variance.

Table 14
*Coefficient Table for OPTEMPO with Trust*

|  |  | Unstandardized Coefficients | | Standardized Coefficients | | |
|---|---|---|---|---|---|---|
|  |  | B | Std. Error | Beta | t | Sig. |
| M1 | (Constant) | 2.063 | .279 |  | 7.394 | .000 |
|  | Caucasian | -.007 | .031 | -.012 | -.249 | .803 |
|  | African American | .007 | .030 | .011 | .112 | .002 |
|  | Other Ethnicity | .001 | .010 | .001 | .102 | .001 |
|  | Education Level | -.102 | .089 | -.061 | -1.146 | .253 |
|  | YOS | .043 | .076 | .036 | .564 | .573 |
|  | MOS | -.104 | .059 | -.094 | -1.762 | .079 |
|  | Gender | .115 | .115 | .054 | 1.003 | .316 |
| M2 | (Constant) | 2.029 | .310 |  | 6.542 | .000 |
|  | Caucasian | -.009 | .034 | -.015 | -.250 | .800 |
|  | African American | .005 | .030 | .011 | .112 | .002 |
|  | Other Ethnicity | -.002 | -.013 | .001 | .102 | .001 |
|  | Education Level | -.103 | .089 | -.063 | -1.150 | .251 |
|  | YOS | .041 | .076 | .033 | .565 | .572 |
|  | MOS | -.104 | .055 | -.094 | -1.750 | .081 |
|  | Gender | .114 | .115 | .053 | .997 | .319 |
|  | **TRUST** | **-.013** | **.051** | **-.011** | **-.258** | **.007** |

Dependent Variable: OPTEMPO

## Quantitative Analysis of Research Question 2

The researcher asked 24 questions using the Commitment scale to measure the level of *Commitment* in captains with regard to their *Intent to Leave* the Army. The researcher conducted bivariate and multivariate statistics on research question two:

RQ2. What is the relationship between organizational commitment with intent to leave the Army?

### Bivariate Correlations between three Dependent Variables with Commitment

According to the 362 students participating in the survey, there was a strong negative correlation between Commitment and ETS, **(-.230)**, as indicated in Table 15 below. Additionally, the research indicated that as Commitment (M = 2.72, SD = 1.53) decreased, ETS (M = 2.74, SD = .848) increased. The research also indicated that Future with Organization (M = 1.68, SD = .958) had a strong correlation with Commitment. OPTEMPO (M = 1.81, SD = .719) appeared insignificant. Table 15 shows the significance between the three dependent variables with the independent variable, Commitment.

Table 15

*Bivariate Correlations between Dependent Variables with Commitment using Pearson*

|  | 1 | 2 | 3 | 4 |
|---|---|---|---|---|
| 1.  ETS | 1 | -.182** | -047 | -.230** |
| 2.  Future  with Organization |  | 1 | .323** | .352** |
| 3.  OPTEMPO |  |  | 1 | -.007 |
| 4.  Commitment |  |  |  | 1 |

*Bold** = significance p<.01*

*Coefficient Table for ETS with Commitment*

Hierarchical multiple regression analysis was performed. Results of the regression analysis provided confirmation for the research hypothesis. Beta coefficients for **Commitment was, β = -.209, t = 3.919, p = .000**. The research indicated that Commitment was a statistically significant predictor to **ETS, (p= .000).** The more the intent to ETS, the less Commitment was shown. For model 1, the adjusted *R2* is .014. In model 2, when Commitment is in the model, adjusted *R2* increased from .052 to .066. This model can explain 6.6% of the variance.

Table 16

*Coefficient Table for ETS with Commitment*

| | | Unstandardized Coefficients | | Standardized Coefficients | | |
| --- | --- | --- | --- | --- | --- | --- |
| | | B | Std. Error | Beta | T | Sig. |
| M1 | (Constant) | 2.699 | .255 | | 9.584 | .000 |
| | Caucasian | .013 | .031 | .023 | .403 | .687 |
| | African American | .007 | .030 | .011 | .112 | .002 |
| | Other Ethnicity | .001 | .010 | .001 | .102 | .001 |
| | Education Level | .136 | .082 | .088 | 1.669 | .096 |
| | YOS | .059 | .068 | .053 | .870 | .385 |
| | MOS | .048 | .054 | .047 | .888 | .375 |
| | Gender | -.072 | .105 | -.036 | -.688 | .492 |
| M2 | (Constant) | 3.419 | .247 | | 9.854 | .000 |
| | Caucasian | -.002 | -.028 | .005 | .087 | .931 |
| | African American | .017 | .030 | .011 | .112 | .002 |
| | Other Ethnicity | -.001 | -.016 | .001 | .102 | .001 |
| | Education Level | -.053 | .075 | .034 | .708 | .479 |
| | YOS | .060 | .062 | .054 | .970 | .333 |
| | MOS | .063 | .049 | .061 | 1.270 | .205 |
| | Gender | -.055 | .096 | -.028 | -.569 | .569 |
| | **Commitment** | **.143** | **.036** | **-.209** | **3.919** | **.000** |

a. Dependent Variable: ETS

*Coefficient Table for Future with Organization and Commitment*

Hierarchical multiple regression analysis was performed. Results of the regression analysis provided confirmation for the research hypothesis. Beta coefficients for **Commitment was, β = -.117, t = -2.157, p = .002**. The research indicated that Commitment was not a statistically significant predictor to Future with Organization, **(p= .002).** The regression further provided that Commitment had a negative effect on MOS and Education Level. For model 1, the adjusted *R2* is .001, in model 2, when Commitment is in added, adjusted *R2* increases .012 to .013. This model can explain 1.3% of the variance.

Table 17

*Coefficient Table for Future with Organization and Commitment*

|  |  | Unstandardized Coefficients | | Standardized Coefficients | | |
|---|---|---|---|---|---|---|
|  |  | B | Std. Error | Beta | | |
| M1 | (Constant) | 2.027 | .272 | | 7.463 | .000 |
|  | Caucasian | -.013 | .033 | -.022 | -.387 | .699 |
|  | African American | .007 | .030 | .011 | .112 | .002 |
|  | Other Ethnicity | .001 | .011 | .000 | .102 | .001 |
|  | Education Level | -.106 | .089 | -.063 | -1.199 | .231 |
|  | YOS | .024 | .068 | .020 | .348 | .728 |
|  | MOS | -.105 | .059 | -.095 | -1.782 | .076 |
|  | Gender | .120 | .114 | .056 | 1.047 | .296 |

| | | B | Std. Error | Beta | T | Sig. |
|---|---|---|---|---|---|---|
| M2 | (Constant) | 2.146 | .276 | | 7.781 | .000 |
| | Caucasian | -.013 | .033 | -.021 | -.380 | .704 |
| | African American | .007 | .030 | .011 | .112 | .002 |
| | Other Ethnicity | .001 | .010 | .001 | .102 | .001 |
| | Education Level | -.095 | .088 | -.056 | -1.070 | .285 |
| | YOS | -.062 | -.070 | .052 | .888 | .375 |
| | MOS | -.107 | .059 | -.096 | -1.814 | .070 |
| | Gender | .120 | .114 | .056 | 1.055 | .292 |
| | **Commitment** | **-.087** | **.040** | **-.117** | **-2.157** | **.002** |

a. Dependent Variable: Future with Organization

Hierarchical multiple regression analysis was performed. Results of the regression analysis provided confirmation for the research hypothesis. Beta coefficients for **Commitment was, $\beta$= -.118, t= -2.184, p= .000**. The research indicated that Commitment was not statistically significant predictor to Future with Organization, **(p= .000).** For model 1, the adjusted $R2$ is .018. In model 2, when Commitment is in the model, adjusted $R2$ increases .028 to .046. This model can explain 4.6% of the variance, see Table 18 below.

Table 18
*Coefficient Table for OPTEMPO with Commitment*

| | | Unstandardized Coefficients | | Standardized Coefficients | | |
|---|---|---|---|---|---|---|
| | | B | Std. Error | Beta | T | Sig. |
| M1 | (Constant) | 1.415 | .211 | | 6.709 | .000 |
| | Caucasian | .016 | .026 | .034 | .600 | .549 |
| | African American | .007 | .030 | .011 | .112 | .002 |
| | Other Ethnicity | .001 | .010 | .001 | .102 | .001 |
| | Education Level | .059 | .069 | .045 | .856 | .393 |
| | YOS | .112 | .053 | .120 | 2.123 | .034 |
| | MOS | .050 | .046 | .057 | 1.084 | .279 |
| | Gender | .099 | .089 | .059 | 1.113 | .266 |

| M2 | | | | | | | |
|---|---|---|---|---|---|---|---|
| | (Constant) | 1.508 | .214 | | | 7.046 | .000 |
| | Caucasian | .016 | .026 | .034 | .613 | | .540 |
| | African American | .007 | .030 | .011 | .112 | | .002 |
| | Other Ethnicity | -.001 | .010 | .001 | .102 | | .001 |
| | Education Level | -.050 | .069 | -.038 | -.725 | | .469 |
| | YOS | -.143 | .054 | .152 | 2.621 | | .009 |
| | MOS | .049 | .046 | .056 | 1.066 | | .287 |
| | Gender | .099 | .088 | .059 | 1.122 | | .262 |
| | **Commitment** | **-.068** | **.031** | **-.118** | **-2.184** | | **.000** |

a. Dependent Variable: Too many deployments

## Quantitative Analysis of Research Question 3

The researcher used eight of the ten questions on the Intent to Leave scale in order to measure the level of intent in captains on leaving the military. Two questions were omitted due to redundancy with the other questions. The researcher conducted bivariate and multivariate statistics on the following research question:

RQ3. What is the relationship between Leader Actions with Intent to Leave the military?

## Bivariate Correlations between three Dependent Variables with Leader Actions

ETS (M = 2.74, SD = .848) and Future with Organization (M = 1.77, SD = .918) have a significant negative correlation with each other according to the 362 students participating in the survey. OPTEMPO (M = 1.81, SD = .719) and Leader Actions (M = 1.28, SD = .451) does not show a significant correlation. Table 19 shows the significance between the three dependent variables with the independent variable, *Leader Actions*.

Table 19

*Bivariate Correlations between three DVs with Leader Actions using Pearson*

|  | 1 | 2 | 3 | 4 |
|---|---|---|---|---|
| 1. ETS | 1 | .-248** | -047 | - .057 |
| 2. Future with Organization | | 1 | .254** | .090 |
| 3. OPTEMPO | | | 1 | -.001 |
| 4. Leader Actions | | | | 1 |

Bold** = significance p<.01

*Coefficient for ETS with Leader Action*

Hierarchical multiple regression analysis was performed. Results of the regression analysis provided confirmation for the research hypothesis. Beta coefficients for *Leader Action* was, **β = -.060, t = -1.132, p = .258.** The research indicated that *Leader Action* was not a statistically significant predictor to Intent to Leave, (p= .258). For model 1, the adjusted *R2* is .005. In model 2, when *leader action* is in the model, adjusted *R2* increases by .004 to .009. This model can explain .01% of the variance.

Table 20

*Coefficient for ETS with Leader Action*

|  |  | Unstandardized Coefficients | | Standardized Coefficients | | |
|---|---|---|---|---|---|---|
|  |  | B | Std. Error | Beta | t | Sig. |
| M1 | (Constant) | 2.550 | .252 | | 1.136 | .000 |
|  | Caucasian | -.005 | .031 | -.009 | -.167 | .868 |
|  | African American | .007 | .030 | .011 | .112 | .002 |
|  | Other Ethnicity | .006 | .010 | .001 | .102 | .001 |
|  | Education Level | .121 | .082 | .078 | 1.479 | .140 |
|  | YOS | -.013 | .063 | -.012 | -.204 | .839 |
|  | MOS | .048 | .055 | .047 | .886 | .376 |
|  | Gender | -.049 | .106 | -.025 | -.459 | .647 |

| | | B | Std. Error | Beta | t | Sig. |
|---|---|---|---|---|---|---|
| M2 | (Constant) | 2.585 | .256 | | 1.116 | .000 |
| | Caucasian | -.003 | .031 | -.005 | -.093 | .926 |
| | African American | .007 | .030 | .011 | .112 | .002 |
| | Other Ethnicity | -.001 | .010 | .001 | .102 | .001 |
| | Education Level | -.134 | .082 | .087 | 1.627 | .105 |
| | YOS | -.011 | .063 | -.010 | -.181 | .856 |
| | MOS | .042 | .055 | .041 | .761 | .447 |
| | Gender | -.041 | .106 | -.021 | -.387 | .699 |
| | **Leader Actions** | **-.020** | **.018** | **-.060** | **-1.132** | **.258** |

a. Dependent Variable: ETS

*Coefficient Table for Future with Organization and Leader Action*

Hierarchical multiple regression analysis was performed. Results of the regression analysis provided confirmation for the research hypothesis. Beta coefficients for *Leader Action* was, **β = .091, t = 1.729, p = .085**. The researcher saw that Leader Action was **not** a statistically significant predictor to Intent to Leave, (p= .085). For model 1, the adjusted *R2* is .002. In model 2, when Leader Action is in the model, adjusted *R2* increases by .007 to .009. This model can explain .01% of the variance.

Table 21

*Coefficient Table for Future with Organization and Leader Action*

| | | Unstandardized Coefficients | | Standardized Coefficients | | |
|---|---|---|---|---|---|---|
| | | B | Std. Error | Beta | t | Sig. |
| M1 | (Constant) | 2.027 | .272 | | 7.463 | .000 |
| | Education Level | -.106 | .089 | -.063 | -1.199 | .231 |
| | Caucasian | .013 | .033 | -.022 | -.387 | .699 |
| | African American | .007 | .030 | .011 | .112 | .002 |
| | Other Ethnicity | .003 | .010 | .001 | .102 | .001 |
| | MOS | -.105 | .059 | -.095 | -1.782 | .076 |
| | Gender | .120 | .114 | .056 | 1.047 | .296 |
| | YOS | .024 | .068 | .020 | .348 | .728 |

| | | B | Std. Error | Beta | t | Sig. |
|---|---|---|---|---|---|---|
| M2 | (Constant) | 1.949 | .276 | | 7.065 | .000 |
| | Education Level | -.120 | .089 | -.072 | -1.354 | .177 |
| | Caucasian | -.017 | .033 | -.029 | -.506 | .613 |
| | African American | .011 | .030 | .011 | .112 | .003 |
| | Other Ethnicity | .003 | .011 | .004 | .102 | -.001 |
| | MOS | .098 | .059 | .089 | 1.662 | .097 |
| | Gender | .112 | .114 | .052 | .984 | .326 |
| | YOS | -027 | .068 | .022 | .390 | .697 |
| | **Leader Actions** | **.034** | **.020** | **.091** | **1.729** | **.085** |

a. Dependent Variable: Future with Organization

*Coefficient Table for OPTEMPO with Leader Action*

Hierarchical multiple regression analysis was performed. Results of the regression analysis provided confirmation for the research hypothesis. Beta coefficients for *Leader Action* was, **β = .007, t = .132, p = .895**. The researcher saw that *Leader Action* was <u>not</u> a statistically significant predictor to Intent to Leave, **(p= .895).** For model 1, the adjusted *R2* is .018. In model 2, when *Leader Action* is in the model, adjusted *R2* increases by .015 to .033. Table 19 can explain 3.3% of the variance.

Table 22

*Coefficient Table for OPTEMPO with Leader Action*

| | | Unstandardized Coefficients | | Standardized Coefficients | | |
|---|---|---|---|---|---|---|
| | | B | Std. Error | Beta | t | Sig. |
| M1 | (Constant) | 1.415 | .211 | | 6.709 | .000 |
| | Education Level | -.059 | .069 | -.045 | -.856 | .393 |
| | Caucasian | .016 | .026 | .034 | .600 | .549 |
| | African American | .007 | .030 | .011 | .112 | .002 |
| | Other Ethnicity | .001 | .010 | .001 | .102 | .001 |
| | MOS | .050 | .046 | .057 | 1.084 | .279 |
| | Gender | .099 | .089 | .059 | 1.113 | .266 |
| | YOS | .112 | .053 | .120 | 2.123 | .034 |

| | | | | | | |
|---|---|---|---|---|---|---|
| M2 | (Constant) | 1.420 | .215 | | 6.606 | .000 |
| | Education Level | -.063 | .069 | -.048 | -.913 | .362 |
| | Caucasian | .015 | .026 | .034 | .594 | .553 |
| | African American | .007 | .030 | .011 | .112 | .002 |
| | Other Ethnicity | -.001 | .010 | .001 | .102 | .001 |
| | MOS | .052 | .046 | .060 | 1.137 | .256 |
| | Gender | .095 | .089 | .057 | 1.075 | .283 |
| | YOS | -.110 | .053 | .117 | 2.067 | .039 |
| | **Leader actions** | **.002** | **.015** | **.007** | **.132** | **.895** |

Dependent Variable: OPTEMPO

Bivariate Correlations for three Dependent Variables with three Independent Variables. Table 23 displays all levels of significance between the three dependent variables with the independent variables.

Table 23
*Bivariate Correlations for three Dependent Variables with three Independent Variables*

| | | 1 | 2 | 3 | 4 | 5 | 6 |
|---|---|---|---|---|---|---|---|
| 1. | ETS | 1 | -.248** | -047 | .085 | -.421** | -.057 |
| 2. | Future with Organization | | 1 | .254** | .021 | .585** | .900 |
| 3. | OPTEMPO | | | 1 | -.051 | .330** | -.001 |
| 4. | Trust | | | | 1 | -.242** | .068 |
| 5. | Commitment | | | | | 1 | .058 |
| 6. | Leader Action | | | | | | 1 |

*Bold** = significance p<.01*

## Multivariate Analysis

For this section, the researcher performed multiple regressions on the three dependent variables focusing on the three independent variables.

## Results of ETS with three Independent Variables

Hierarchical multiple regression analysis was performed. Results of the regression analysis provided confirmation for the research hypothesis. Beta coefficients for trust was, $\beta$ = .074, $t$ = 1,393, $p$ =.164; **Commitment: $\beta$ = .200, $t$ = 1.699, $p$ =.000** and Leader Actions: $\beta$ = -.078, $t$ = -1.478, $p$ =.140. The analysis revealed that *Trust* and *Leader Action* were not statistically significant, only *Commitment* was significant. Research indicated that as levels of *Commitment* decrease, *ETS* increases. Conversely, the more the intent to ETS, the less *Commitment* was shown. The regression analysis revealed gender, YOS, ethnic background and education had insignificant impact on ETS. For model 1, the adjusted *R2* is .015. In model 2, when all three independent variables are in the model, adjusted *R2* increases to .170. This model can explain 1.8% variance.

Table 24

*Coefficient table for ETS with three Independent Variables*

| | | Unstandardized Coefficients | | Standardized Coefficients | | |
| --- | --- | --- | --- | --- | --- | --- |
| | | B | Std. Error | Beta | t | Sig. |
| M1 | (Constant) | 2.550 | .252 | | 1.136 | .000 |
| | Education Level | .121 | .082 | .078 | 1.479 | .140 |
| | Caucasian | -.005 | .031 | -.009 | -.167 | .868 |
| | African American | .007 | .030 | .011 | .112 | .002 |
| | Other Ethnicity | .001 | .010 | .001 | .102 | .001 |
| | MOS | .048 | .055 | .047 | .886 | .376 |
| | Gender | -.049 | .106 | -.025 | -.459 | .647 |
| | YOS | -.013 | .063 | -.012 | -.204 | .839 |
| M2 | (Constant) | 2.213 | .289 | | 7.650 | .000 |
| | Education Level | .111 | .081 | .072 | 1.378 | .169 |
| | Caucasian | -.002 | .030 | -.004 | -.073 | .942 |
| | African American | .007 | .030 | .011 | .112 | .002 |
| | Other Ethnicity | .001 | .010 | .001 | .102 | .001 |
| | MOS | .047 | .054 | .046 | .878 | .380 |
| | Gender | -.041 | .104 | -.021 | -.401 | .689 |

| | | | | | |
|---|---|---|---|---|---|
| YOS | -.086 | .065 | -.078 | -1.336 | .183 |
| TRUST | .093 | .067 | .074 | 1.393 | .164 |
| **COMMITMENT** | **.136** | **.037** | **.200** | **1.699** | **.000** |
| LEADER ACTION | -.026 | .018 | -.078 | -1.481 | .140 |

Dependent Variable: ETS

*Future with Organization and three Independent Variables*

Hierarchical multiple regression analysis was performed. Results of the regression analysis provided confirmation for the research hypothesis. Beta coefficients for *trust* was, $\beta$ = **.101**, *t* = **2.342**, *p* =**.001**; *Commitment*: $\beta$ = **.601**, *t* = **1.784**, *p* =**.000** and for *Leader Action*: $\beta$ = .022, *t* = .512, *p* =.609. The regression further revealed ethnic background, YOS, MOS had negative impacts on Future with Organization. The research showed that gender, and age had a positive effect on Future with Organization. Both **trust (p=.001),** and **commitment (p=.000),** were statistically significant. Research showed that as levels of *Future with Organization* increased as did the levels of *Trust*. Research also showed that higher levels of Commitment were seen with the higher levels of Future with Organization. For model 1, the adjusted $R_2$ was .015. This model can explain 15% variance. In model 2, when all three independent variables were in the model, adjusted $R_2$ increased by 16%. This model can explain 3.1% variance.

Table 25

*Future with Organization and three Independent Variables*

| | | Unstandardized Coefficients | | Standardized Coefficients | | |
|---|---|---|---|---|---|---|
| | | B | Std. Error | Beta | t | Sig. |
| M1 | (Constant) | 2.027 | .272 | | 7.463 | .000 |
| | Gender | .120 | .114 | .056 | 1.047 | .296 |
| | YOS | .024 | .068 | .020 | .348 | .728 |
| | Education Level | -.106 | .089 | -.063 | -1.199 | .231 |
| | Caucasian | -.013 | .033 | -.022 | -.387 | .699 |

| | | | | | | |
|---|---|---|---|---|---|---|
| | African American | .007 | .030 | .011 | .112 | .002 |
| | Other Ethnicity | .001 | .010 | .001 | .102 | .001 |
| | MOS | -.105 | .059 | -.095 | -1.782 | .076 |
| | | | | | | |
| M2 | (Constant) | .546 | .274 | | 1.992 | .047 |
| | Gender | .094 | .092 | .044 | 1.018 | .309 |
| | YOS | -.013 | .056 | -.011 | -.240 | .811 |
| | Education Level | .008 | .072 | .005 | .115 | .908 |
| | Caucasian | -.001 | .027 | -.002 | -.050 | .960 |
| | African American | .007 | .030 | .011 | .112 | .002 |
| | Other Ethnicity | .001 | .010 | .001 | .102 | .001 |
| | MOS | -.120 | .048 | -.108 | -2.508 | .013 |
| | **TRUST** | **.140** | **.060** | **.101** | **2.324** | **.001** |
| | **COMMITMENT** | **.599** | **.043** | **.601** | **1.784** | **.000** |
| | LEADER ACTION | .008 | .016 | .022 | .512 | .609 |

Dependent Variable: Future with Organization

Hierarchical multiple regression analysis was performed. Results of the regression analysis provided confirmation for the research hypothesis. Beta coefficients for Trust was, $\beta$ = -.058, $t$ = -1.093, $p$ =.275; Commitment: **$\beta$= -.114, $t$ = -2.100, $p$ =.000** and Leader Action: $\beta$ = .018, $t$ = .340, $p$ =.734. The regression revealed *trust* and c*ommitment* had a negative effect on Too Many Deployments. The regression further revealed *Trust*, and c*ommitment* and education level had negative impacts on OPTEMPO. ***Commitment was* statistically significant, p=.000**. The research indicated that gender, age, and MOS were significant predictors to OPTEMPO. For model 1, the adjusted $R_2$ is .017. This model can explain 1.7% variance. In model 2, when all three independent variables are in the model, adjusted $R_2$ increased by .024. This model can explain 4.1% variance.

Table 26.
*OPTEMPO with three Independent Variables*

|    |                   | Unstandardized Coefficients | | Standardized Coefficients | | |
| --- | --- | --- | --- | --- | --- | --- |
|    |                   | B | Std. Error | Beta | T | Sig. |
| M1 | (Constant)        | 1.415 | .211 |      | 6.709 | .000 |
|    | Gender            | .099 | .089 | .059 | 1.113 | .266 |
|    | YOS               | .112 | .053 | .120 | 2.123 | .034 |
|    | Education Level   | -.059 | .069 | -.045 | -.856 | .393 |
|    | Caucasian         | .016 | .026 | .034 | .600 | .549 |
|    | African American  | .007 | .030 | .011 | .112 | .002 |
|    | Other Ethnicity   | .001 | .010 | .001 | .102 | .001 |
|    | MOS               | .050 | .046 | .057 | 1.084 | .279 |
| M2 | (Constant)        | 1.636 | .247 |      | 6.628 | .000 |
|    | Gender            | .096 | .088 | .057 | 1.086 | .278 |
|    | YOS               | .149 | .055 | .159 | 2.695 | .007 |
|    | Education Level   | -.051 | .069 | -.039 | -.744 | .458 |
|    | Caucasian         | .015 | .026 | .033 | .580 | .562 |
|    | African American  | .007 | .030 | .011 | .112 | .002 |
|    | Other Ethnicity   | .001 | .010 | .001 | .102 | .001 |
|    | MOS               | .049 | .046 | .056 | 1.068 | .286 |
|    | TRUST             | -.062 | .057 | -.058 | -1.093 | .275 |
|    | **COMMITMENT**    | **-.066** | **.031** | **-.114** | **-2.100** | **.000** |
|    | LEADER ACTION     | .005 | .015 | .018 | .340 | .734 |

Dependent Variable: OPTEMPO

*Bivariate Correlations between three Dependent Variables with Covariates*

This table presents the covariates that have the strongest impact on the three dependent variables. The researcher points out a couple of observations about the covariates, specifically, Education, YOS and Future with Organization all have a significant impact on OPTEMPO. ETS has a significant negative correlation with Future with Organization.

Table 27

*Bivariate Correlations for three Dependent Variables with Covariates using Spearman*

|  | 1 | 2 | 3 | 4 | 5 | 6 | 7 | 8 |
|---|---|---|---|---|---|---|---|---|
| MOS | 1 | .-073 | -0.048 | 0.072 | 0.101 | 0.041 | -0.083 | 0.071 |
| Ethnic Background |  | 1 | 0.003 | **.354**\*\* | 0.057 | -0.018 | -0.015 | 0.075 |
| Education |  |  | 1 | -0.077 | -0.057 | 0.078 | -0.064 | **-0.112\*** |
| YOS |  |  |  | 1 | 0.105 | -0.02 | 0.016 | **.146\*\*** |
| Gender |  |  |  |  | 1 | -0.026 | 0.051 | 0.082 |
| ETS |  |  |  |  |  | 1 | **-.248\*\*** | -0.047 |
| Future with Organization |  |  |  |  |  |  | 1 | **.313\*\*** |
| OPTEMPO |  |  |  |  |  |  |  | 1 |

**Bold\*\*** Correlation is significant at p<0.01 level

**Bold\*** Correlation is significant at p<0.05 level

Table 28

*Bivariate Correlations for three Independent Variables with Covariates using Spearman*

|  | 1 | 2 | 3 | 4 | 5 | 6 | 7 | 8 |
|---|---|---|---|---|---|---|---|---|
| 1. MOS | 1 | .-075 | -0.044 | 0.066 | 0.103 | -0.046 | 0.004 | 0.016 |
| 2. Ethnic Background |  | 1 | -0.010 | **.351\*\*** | 0.054 | -0.035 | 0.093 | 0.047 |
| 3. Education |  |  | 1 | -0.077 | -0.053 | 0.058 | 0.031 | **-0.132\*** |
| 4. YOS |  |  |  | 1 | 0.105 | -0.02 | **.179\*\*** | **.146\*\*** |
| 5. Gender |  |  |  |  | 1 | -0.005 | 0.016 | 0.082 |
| 6. Trust |  |  |  |  |  | 1 | **.229\*\*** | -0.047 |
| 7. Commitment |  |  |  |  |  |  | 1 | **.217\*\*** |
| 8. Leader actions |  |  |  |  |  |  |  | 1 |

**Bold\*\*** Correlation is significant at p<0.01 level

**Bold\*** Correlation is significant at p<0.05 level

## Multivariate Analysis

For this section, the researcher performed multiple regressions on the three independent variables focusing on the covariates. Hierarchical multiple regression analysis was performed. Results of the **ETS** regression analysis provided confirmation for the research hypothesis. Beta coefficients for *Trust* was, $\beta=.074$, $t = 1.393$, $p =.164$;

*Commitment* **was, β=.200, *t* = 3.699, *p* =.000**; *Leader Action* was, β=.078, *t* = 1.481,

*p* =.140. Gender, YOS, education all had negative and insignificant effects on ETS.

Table 29

*Results of ETS with three Independent Variables*

|  |  | Unstandardized Coefficients | | Standardized Coefficients | | |
|---|---|---|---|---|---|---|
|  |  | B | Std. Error | Beta | t | Sig. |
| M1 | (Constant) | 2.550 | .252 |  | 1.136 | .000 |
|  | Gender | -.049 | .106 | -.025 | -.459 | .647 |
|  | YOS | -.013 | .063 | -.012 | -.204 | .839 |
|  | Education Level | .121 | .082 | .078 | 1.479 | .140 |
|  | Caucasian | -.005 | .031 | -.009 | -.167 | .868 |
|  | African American | .007 | .030 | .011 | .112 | .002 |
|  | Other Ethnicity | .001 | .010 | .001 | .102 | .001 |
|  | MOS | .048 | .055 | .047 | .886 | .376 |
| M2 | (Constant) | 2.213 | .289 |  | 7.650 | .000 |
|  | Gender | -.041 | .104 | -.021 | -.401 | .689 |
|  | YOS | -.086 | .065 | -.078 | -1.336 | .183 |
|  | Education Level | .111 | .081 | .072 | 1.378 | .169 |
|  | Caucasian | -.002 | .030 | -.004 | -.073 | .942 |
|  | African American | .007 | .030 | .011 | .112 | .002 |
|  | Other Ethnicity | .004 | .013 | .001 | .102 | .001 |
|  | MOS | .047 | .054 | .046 | .878 | .380 |
|  | TRUST | .093 | .067 | .074 | 1.393 | .164 |
|  | **COMMITMENT** | **.136** | **.037** | **.200** | **3.699** | **.000** |
|  | LEADER ACTION | -.026 | .018 | -.078 | -1.481 | .140 |

Dependent Variable: ETS

*Future with Organization with three Independent Variables*

Hierarchical multiple regression analysis was performed. Results of the regression analysis provided confirmation for the research hypothesis. Future with Organization for

*Trust* was, β = .023, *t* = .429, *p* =.668; *Commitment* **was, β =.-126, *t* = -2.300, *p*=.001**;

*Leader Action* was, β = 098, *t* = 1.847, *p* =.066. Gender, ethnicities, education, and MOS had negative effects on *Future with Organization*. In model 2, when the researcher added

the three independent variables, *commitment* was shown statistically significant.

Table 30

*Results of Future with Organization and three Independent Variables*

| | | Unstandardized Coefficients | | Standardized Coefficients | | |
|---|---|---|---|---|---|---|
| | | B | Std. Error | Beta | t | Sig. |
| M1 | (Constant) | 2.027 | .272 | | 7.463 | .000 |
| | Gender | .120 | .114 | .056 | 1.047 | .296 |
| | TIS | .024 | .068 | .020 | .348 | .728 |
| | Education Level | -.106 | .089 | -.063 | -1.199 | .231 |
| | Caucasian | -.013 | .033 | -.022 | -.387 | .699 |
| | African American | .007 | .030 | .011 | .112 | .002 |
| | Other Ethnicity | .001 | .010 | .001 | .102 | .001 |
| | MOS | -.105 | .059 | -.095 | -1.782 | .076 |
| M2 | (Constant) | 2.004 | .317 | | 6.317 | .000 |
| | Gender | .112 | .114 | .052 | .987 | .324 |
| | TIS | .064 | .071 | .053 | .900 | .369 |
| | Education Level | -.110 | .089 | -.066 | -1.246 | .214 |
| | Caucasian | -.017 | .033 | -.028 | -.502 | .616 |
| | African American | .007 | .030 | .011 | .112 | .002 |
| | Other Ethnicity | .001 | .010 | .001 | .102 | .001 |
| | MOS | -.098 | .059 | -.088 | -1.663 | .097 |
| | TRUST | .031 | .073 | .023 | .429 | .668 |
| | **COMMITMENT** | **-.093** | **.040** | **-.126** | **-2.300** | **.001** |
| | LEADER ACTIONS | .036 | .020 | .098 | 1.847 | .066 |

Dependent Variable: Future with organization

*OPTEMPO with three Independent Variables*

Hierarchical multiple regression analysis was performed. Results of the regression

analysis provided confirmation for the research hypothesis. Beta coefficients for

Education had negative effects on Too Many Deployments. The research showed all other covariates were statistically insignificant. In model 2, when the researcher added the three independent variables, only *Commitment* **showed a statistical significance, β= -.114, *t*= 2.100, *p*=.001.**

Table 31

*Results of OPTEMPO with three Independent Variables*

|  |  | Unstandardized Coefficients | | Standardized Coefficients |  |  |
|---|---|---|---|---|---|---|
|  |  | B | Std. Error | Beta | t | Sig. |
| M1 | (Constant) | 1.415 | .211 |  | 6.709 | .000 |
|  | Gender | .099 | .089 | .059 | 1.113 | .266 |
|  | TIS | .112 | .053 | .120 | 2.123 | .034 |
|  | Education Level | -.059 | .069 | -.045 | -.856 | .393 |
|  | Caucasian | .016 | .026 | .034 | .600 | .549 |
|  | African American | .007 | .030 | .011 | .112 | .002 |
|  | Other Ethnicity | .001 | .010 | .001 | .102 | .001 |
|  | MOS | .050 | .046 | .057 | 1.084 | .279 |
| M2 | (Constant) | 1.636 | .247 |  | 6.628 | .000 |
|  | Gender | .096 | .088 | .057 | 1.086 | .278 |
|  | TIS | .149 | .055 | .159 | 2.695 | .007 |
|  | Education Level | -.051 | .069 | -.039 | -.744 | .458 |
|  | Caucasian | .015 | .026 | .033 | .580 | .562 |
|  | African American | .007 | .030 | .011 | .112 | .002 |
|  | Other Ethnicity | .001 | .010 | .001 | .102 | .001 |
|  | MOS | .049 | .046 | .056 | 1.068 | .286 |
|  | TRUST | -.062 | .057 | -.058 | -1.093 | .275 |
|  | **COMMITMENT** | **-.066** | **.031** | **-.114** | **-2.100** | **.001** |
|  | LEADER ACTION | .005 | .015 | .018 | .340 | .734 |

Dependent Variable: OPTEMPO

**Summary Findings for Research Questions**

Findings for Question 1

The researcher ran multiple regression statistics and bivariate correlation to analyze the relationship between *Trust*, *Commitment*, and *Leader Actions* with the *Intent to Leave* the Army. For all of the research questions, the researcher ran the same analysis. For research question one, (*What is the relationship between organizational trust with intent to leave the Army?*). The regression analysis determined that *trust* had a strong statistical relationship to *intent to leave* for the sampled population of Army captains.

In this study, a relationship between *trust* and *intent to leave* was one of the hypotheses tested. A relationship between *trust* and *intent* for officers leaving the Army, is confirmed. *Trust* is directly related to the *intent* for junior officers' leaving the Army and was accepted when tested in looking for a relationship between trust and intent to leave. In determining if there was a relationship between trust and intent to leave, the following hypothesis is rejected Ho: "There is no relationship between trust and intent for captains to leave the Army."

The results illustrated a significant level of relationship between trust and intent to leave the military. A regression analysis demonstrated a 15.1% of the variance in intent to leave can be explained by trust in leadership through this study. This result is similar to results seen in Milligan (2003) and Vadell (2008).

After performing hierarchical multiple regression analysis, results provided confirmation for the research hypothesis. The researcher saw that *trust* was a statistically significant predictor to *Intent to Leave*. ETS has a strong negative correlation at the .01 level with Future with Organization, (M = 2.74, SD = .848). Future with Organization (M = 1.77, SD = .918) is clearly more significant predictor than OPTEMPO (M = 1.76, SD =

.646) in relation to Trust, as reported by the students participating in the survey. Trust (M = 2.22, SD = .733) is a significant predictor to the significance of Future with Organization. **Beta coefficients for ETS and *trust* was, β =.019, *t* = 2.083, *p* = .008.** The researcher saw that *trust* was a statistically significant predictor to ETS and the *Intent to Leave*, **p=.008**. For model M1, the adjusted $R_2$ is -.007.

This research builds a stronger case that exists within many organizations and within the U.S. Army. *Trust* holds statistically significant correlations with intentions of leaving an organization. Literature and previous studies have demonstrated trust as a main attribute to transformational leadership. The Department of Defense has looked into this trend of transformational leadership as style for the military in order to step-up for future challenges, technological advances, and an increase of operations throughout the world. As the military stretches it forces throughout the world, trust seems to be a developing factor in culture and relationships between leaders and their subordinates. As previous scholars have suggested, trust as a key to "successful organizational outcomes including cooperative behavior, reduced conflict, improved communications, effective crisis response and improved performance" (Milligan, 2003, p. 155) in the military.

When the Army Chief of Staff stated that military leadership must encourage risk taking and failure in the pursuit of new ideas, he was in fact trumpeting the requirement for building stronger trusting relationships between military leaders and subordinates (2014).

Findings for Question 2

For research question two, a hierarchical linear regression determined *Commitment* had a strong statistical relationship to *intent to leave* with officers in the U.S. Army. The second research question in this study is "What is the relationship between organizational commitment and intent to leave the Army?" In order to examine this question the following hypotheses were proposed: What is the relationship between organizational *commitment* with *intent to leave* the Army? A hierarchical linear regression determined that *commitment* had a strong statistical relationship to *intent to leave* for the sampled population of captains in the Army.

The current study demonstrated a relationship between commitment and intent to leave the military. The following hypotheses, H2. There is a relationship between organizational *commitment* and *intent* for junior officers' leaving the Army was accepted when tested in looking for a relationship between commitment and intent to leave. The following hypothesis was rejected in determining if there was a relationship between trust and commitment: H2o. There is no relationship between organizational commitment and intent for junior officers' leaving the Army. Results from the current testing between the relationship of *commitment* and *intent to leave* were found to be similar to Milligan's study in 2003. Vadell (2008) concluded that the turnover *intent* of Air Force military personnel is consistently related to *commitment*.

In Milligan's (2003) as well as Vadell's (2008) study, there was a similar relationship between *commitment* and *intent to leave*. *Commitment* is considered to be capable of an enhanced organization and job characteristics. As there was an increase in *commitment* there was a direct decrease in the *intent to leave*. This study demonstrated similar results. Some captains clearly stated an emotional attachment to the Army. Milligan (2003) wrote "commitment can be managed and promoted through leadership and human resource practices resulting in greater commitment and less turnover" (p. 150). These captains are most likely not leaving the Army as someone who had less of an attachment with the Army.

Senior leaders must commit to reversing the present thirty-year trend by eliminating systems, which encourage dysfunctional behavior, reward behavior in leaders that fosters functional characteristics and consciously exhibit functional characteristics at their level of influence. If senior leaders intentionally strive to reverse the present paradigms in the U.S. Army, the relationships between officers will improve and the U.S. Army will reap the benefit of greater creativity and commitment across the officer corps.

According to the 362 students participating in the survey, there is a strong negative correlation between Commitment (M = 2.72, SD = 1.53) with ETS (M = 2.74, SD = .848). Future with Organization (M = 1.68, SD = .958) has a strong correlation with Commitment. OPTEMPO appears insignificant, (M = 1.81, SD = .719).

Results of the regression analysis provided confirmation for the research hypothesis. **Beta coefficients for Commitment was, β = -.209, t = 3.919, p = .000**. The researcher confirmed, *Commitment* was a statistically significant predictor to Intent to Leave, **(p= .000).**

The literature suggested a relationship between the supervisor and subordinate is needed in order to provide a positive and influential connection to the organization. Commitment was characterized by an apparent fairness in equity of the suggested relationship in the literature. This research builds a stronger case that exists within many organizations and within the U.S. Army. *Commitment* holds statistically significant correlations with intentions of leaving an organization. The researcher found that *commitment* was a statistically significant predictor to *intent to leave* the military.

Findings for Question 3

For research question three, a hierarchical linear regression determined *Leader Actions* did not have a strong relationship to *intent to leave* with captains in the Army.

ETS (M = 2.74, SD = .848) and Future with Organization (M = 1.77, SD = .918) have a significant negative correlation with each other according to the 362 students participating in the survey. OPTEMPO (M = 1.81, SD = .719) and Leader Actions (M = 1.28, SD = .451) is **not** a significant correlation. The following hypothesis is rejected in determining if there was a relationship between leader action and intent to leave: H3 There is a significant relationship between leader action and intent to leave the Army. The following hypothesis is accepted: H3o There is no significant statistical relationship between *leader actions* and *intent to leave* the Army. The regression revealed $R$ = .060, $R2$ = .009, $F$ ($R$= -1.132, $p$ = .258 for Leader Actions. Results of the regression analysis provided confirmation for the research hypothesis. Beta coefficients were, $\beta$ = -.060, t = -1.132, p = .258. The research indicated that Leader Action was not a significant predictor to *Intent to Leave*, (p= .258).

# CHAPTER 5. DISCUSSION AND IMPLICATIONS OF THE RESEARCH

## Introduction

Conclusion of the research study brought closure with an evaluation of the results, limitations, implications and recommendations for future research. The researcher examined the relationship between *trust, commitment*, and *leader actions* with *intent to leave* the U.S. Army. The constructs follow the theoretical framework of Milligan (2003). The MBCA, Commitment Scales, and the Intent to Leave survey measured the constructs used in this research.

The research depended on the availability of the captains at the Captains Career Course for participation. An anonymous paper survey was administered in this research to a random sample size of 400 captains selected from the student population. The survey was designed for each participant to answer all questions. The final sample size of 362 participants had responded to the research survey, resulting in a 91% response rate used in this research.

The research focused strictly on study population of captains at the Fort Lee, Virginia, Captains Career Course. Two classes run simultaneously, each class has a total of 300 for a grand total of 600. The minimum acceptable sample size was set at 350, maximum was set at 450, and the optimal number was 400.

The students attending the Captains Career Course comprise the sample population. The dependent variable was *intent to leave*. The researcher examined three dependent sub-variables: ETS, Future with Organization, and Too Many Deployments. The independent variables for the study were *trust, commitment,* and *leader actions*. The researcher controlled for the variables using the covariates of gender, age, ethnicity, YOS, education, and MOS. The researcher performed appropriate and necessary dummy coding and recoding on ethnicity and MOS. The previous chapter provided the results of the statistical analysis pertaining to the following research questions:

RQ1. What is the relationship between the trust with intent to leave the Army?

RQ2. What is the relationship between commitment and intent to leave the Army?

RQ3. What is the relationship between leader action and intent to leave the Army?

**Implications of the Research**

Given the fact that there is limited research available on the level of organizational trust in military populations, this research examined the level of trust in Army leadership among Army Captains and measured results against the findings from Milligan's research. The first discussion focused on the question, "What is the relationship between the trust with intent to leave the Army?"

Milligan's Leadership Theory implied that a strong emphasis placed upon trust increased human satisfaction in terms of feeling of accomplishment and as the center of gravity in relation to successful leadership. The study helped determine if MOS, age, gender, education, and YOS have a significant effect on trust, commitment, leader actions with intent to leave the military.

The research findings imply that *trust* and *commitment* are both indicators of officers' *intent to leave* the Army. The purpose of this study was to determine if *trust*, *commitment* and *leader actions* hold a significant relationship with an *intent to leave* the Army. The study derived survey data from captains attending the Captains Career Course, Fort Lee Virginia. From the dimensions that account for the overall intent to leave, the researcher created a survey for the participants. All participants took the survey; ten were partially filled out, illegible and omitted. The research findings concluded that *leader action* is the only construct that has a <u>no</u> statistically significant relationship with the intention to leave the Army.

The current study used Milligan's Theory of Leadership which when applied to the dimensions of military leadership has shown may impact perceptions of trust and commitment which potentially affect intent to leave the military.

**Trust and Intent to Leave**

The <u>first</u> research question in the study, "What is the relationship between *trust* and *intent to leave* the Army?" is defined throughout the entire study. The supported hypothesis: $H_1$: There is a relationship between organizational *trust* with *intent to leave* the Army. The rejected hypothesis: $H_0$. There is no relationship between organizational *trust* with *intent to leave* the Army. The results of this research show a proven statistical significant relationship between *trust* in leadership and *intent to leave* the Army. The research demonstrated that *trust* is one of the reasons that impact the decision officers choose in leaving the Army. $H_{1a}$. *Trust* <u>is</u> directly related to *intent to leave*.

Although there was a statistically significant relationship between *trust* and *intent to leave*, some thought of the current results rise from this data. One idea is a lack of *trust* as a variable in the problem of captains leaving the Army after their initial term of service. Another idea is the decrease of job security as the Army continues decreasing their numbers of active duty members since 2013. As the Islamic State of Iraq and Syria, (ISIS) conflict continues overseas, the Army continues deploying members, despite the downsizing. Operation tempo has increased and while members are being forced out, their duties still need to be fulfilled. The decision of junior officers' leaving the Army may be more complicated and may contain many other variables. Other variables could include the economy, civilian jobs, assignment, location, pay, and overall job satisfaction.

The current study demonstrated that trust is one of the potential issues impacting captains' leaving the Army as it is with captains leaving the Air Force.

The 2014 QDR states that exceptional people with the right skills for the 21st century and attitudes nourished in a culture that encourages bold innovation and leadership are essential to the implementation of its transformation strategy. The literature suggests that distrust destroys innovation while trust is integral to the generation of new ideas and the implementation of those ideas (Clegg et al., 2002).

Within the 2014 Quadrennial Defense Review, the Secretary of Defense calls for a complete transformation of military forces to fight and win through 2025. To achieve this transformation leadership must build trusting relationships through innovative thinking and encouraging risk taking in the pursuit of new ideas and capabilities. The literature suggests that trust and risk taking are inextricably connected, "trust and risk give rise to one another; it is rare to find one without the other" (Milligan 2003).

The research explored the relationship between organizational trust, commitment and intent to leave the military, specifically, "What is the level of trust in senior leadership as reported by Army captains?" Circumstantial information from current Army literature from both CGSC and the Army War College suggest that levels of trust are low among military officers, and are particularly low in mid-career captains. Milligan's study reported the MBCA mean scores of trust to be 3.6 or average. The results of this study were considerably less at 2.8, or below average.

The scoring method was a five point Likert scale with the follow response options: Rarely / Never, Seldom, Occasionally, Usually, and Almost Always. It is important to note that a score of 3.0 on the MBCA scale conveys a response of "Occasionally" and not one of neutrality. As an example of this distinction, not many would consider the fact that nearly 60% of respondents believe that senior leadership usually or less often tells the truth a favorable rating, consistent with Milligan's (2003). On this item (MBCA Item 20), .02% lower, but also consistent with Milligan's study, nearly 23% of the respondents believed that Senior Leadership always or almost always told the truth. Two study participants provided a comment on this issue; on the survey instruments, it was written, "In my opinion an Army "values" violation to me is a character violation" and "once a toxic leader – always a toxic leader." Some mixed feelings shown but still results are statistically significant and display an overall low level of trust toward senior leaders, consistent with not only Milligan's (2003) but also Vadell's (2008).

Similarly, 55% of the respondents believed that Senior Leaders usually or more often play favorites (MBCA Item 11). Trust in leadership in a military environment was evaluated on a system where any score above 3.0 per item is above average and any score below 3.0 is below average. For this research, an average rating among respondents on any given item of 4.5 or higher is excellent; an average score of 4.0 - 4.49 per item is above average or good; an average rating among respondents of 3.5 to 3.99 per item is average; an average rating among respondents of 3.0 to 3.49 per item is below average or marginal and any average score of 2.9 or less is poor.

With this evaluation tool in mind, it was possible to evaluate the question, "What is the level of trust in senior leadership, as reported by Army captains?" In relation to Milligan's (2003) findings where the level of trust in leadership as reported by Air Force captains was an average 3.6, the level of trust reported by Army captains was reported as 2.8 or poor. The researcher ran multiple correlation analysis to determine whether a relationship existed between trust of officers' and senior leadership. A total of nearly

23% stated "always/almost" that senior leaders tell the truth, less than in Milligan's study (25%) in 2003 and in Vadell's study (26%) in 2008.

Maslow's theory of motivation purporting that human beings are motivated by unsatisfied needs, and that certain lower needs have to be satisfied before higher needs can be addressed. Although this research did not address Maslow Hierarchy of needs in the study, the researcher implied it using the constructs of trust and commitment. There was an ill-defined gap in trust as discussed in this research. Measuring the results from Milligan's (2003), and utilizing the same proven validated scales, the research displayed conclusive statistical significance to aid in bridging the gap in trust for future leadership to build upon.

The reported responses showed that 37% of the respondents would most likely stay in the Army, given their current situation. However, the research showed 51% of the respondents thought about leaving the military after their commitment. The research displayed that Trust was a statistically significant predictor to Intent to Leave ($p<.01$). The adjusted R2 was .011. When Trust was added to the model, adjusted R2 increased by.030. Trust can explain 4.1% of the total change in variance.

The results from question one presented in this summary strongly imply that the statistical significant of *trust* is essential to successful leaders and military operations. For research question one, hierarchical multiple regression analysis was performed. Results of the regression analysis provided confirmation for the research hypothesis. The research indicated that *trust* was a statistically significant predictor to *Intent to Leave,* ($p<.01$). "One of the most powerful and efficient organizational tools ever invented is the trusting relationship. With trust and trusting relationships, imperfect plans can be made to work; without trust and trusting relationships even the most perfectly conceived plan can fail"

(Culbert & McDonough, 1986). Military organizations like other types of organizations are dependent on strong interpersonal dynamics and teamwork. This research supports a strong link between *trust* and *intent to leave* an organization.

**Commitment and Intent to Leave**

The <u>second research</u> question "What is the relationship between organizational *commitment* with *intent to leave?*" Hierarchical multiple regression analysis was performed and the results of the regression analysis provided confirmation for the research hypothesis. The research indicated that *commitment* <u>was</u> a statistically significant predictor to *Intent to Leave*, (p=.000).

Aubrey (2013) findings represented a reduced trust and commitment levels exhibited by an organization's members due to toxic leadership and found three prominent outliers. One, when members *no longer trust the leadership to look out for their best interests* they may not only *resist promoting the organization to friends and family* but also *actively campaign against membership to the organization*. Two, retiring members who may have been subjected to toxic leadership may *voice negative opinions about the organization to external and internal stakeholders*. Suggestive intent is that the lack of trust may extend beyond the toxic leader to other members of the organization and result in power struggles. A third finding suggested toxic leadership may lead to *high personnel turnover* as members start to experience *decreased job satisfaction*.

Milligan stated, "*commitment* can be managed and promoted through leadership and human resource practices resulting in greater commitment and less turnover" (2003, p. 150). This current study demonstrated a statistically significant relationship between *commitment* and *intent to leave*.

In examining <u>question two</u>, the following hypotheses are accepted: H2. There is a relationship between *commitment* and the *intent to leave* the Army and H2a. *Commitment* is directly related to *intent to leave* were both accepted when tested in looking for a relationship. The following hypothesis was rejected in determining a relationship between *commitment* and *intent to leave*: H2o. There is no relationship between *commitment* and the *intent to leave* commitment in officers' staying in the Army.

In Vadell's (2008) study, results were similar as there was a relationship between *commitment* and *intent to leave*. Vadell reported that as there was an increase in *commitment*, there was a direct decrease in the *intent to leave*. The current study demonstrated similar results. Some officers' clearly stated an emotional attachment to the Army. These individuals are most likely not leaving the military as if someone who had less of an attachment to the Army. The literature suggests a relationship between the supervisor and subordinate is needed to provide a positive and influential connection to the organization.

Commitment was represented by a perceived fairness and equity of the suggested relationship in the literature. Approximately 61% of officers' in the Army reported low or very low levels of *commitment*. This *commitment* is considered to be developed through socialization efforts and a shared vision. The literature demonstrates this in military training and history. This is commonly seen in basic training for enlisted members and field training for officers depending on their commissioning source.

The statistically significant level of *commitment* in this study demonstrated that even though the military is increasing some benefits and even a yearly pay increase, there are still rising *commitment* concerns. This may be a contribution of the increased chance of officers losing their jobs as the Army conducts continued officer separation boards while simultaneously increasing deployments due to the ongoing situation with ISIS in Iraq and Syria. With the recent White House announcement of boots on the ground in Syria, this contradicts President Obama's original pledge to the American public that there will not be an increased military involvement to deal with ISIS.

**Leader Actions and Intent to Leave**

The third research question, "What is the relationship between *Leader Action* and *intent to leave* the Army?" The following hypothesis was accepted: H3o: There is not a relationship between *Leader Action* and *intent* for officers' leaving the Army. Hierarchical multiple regression analysis was performed and the results of the regression analysis provided confirmation for the research. The researcher saw that *Leader Action* was not a statistically significant predictor to *Intent to Leave*, (p= .258). *Leader action* was the least statistically significant of the three independent variables examined in this study. Among officers surveyed, *leader actions* were reported to be the least of the three independent variables leading to an intention to quit than were the other two IVs, *trust* or *commitment*. "Effective Leadership has always been important factor in determining whether young officers will remain within our ranks or not. The pace of operations over the past 10 years has placed added pressure on leader development, and although they add to our versatility, our modular structures have altered the traditional pattern of senior and subordinate relationships. We're doing well, but never good enough in this important aspect of our profession." Gen. Martin Dempsey.

Regardless, *leader actions* play a role in the outcomes of their subordinates effective must share the vision of the Army with its officers and help them understand the importance of that vision in order to gain *commitment* in achieving the vision (Klein,

2007). The military is looking towards building this stronger *commitment* as senior leaders push their transformational thought of leadership to younger officers.

**Conclusion**

The researcher's interpretation is grounded in the theory of Milligan which implies, when the subordinates share the leader's vision; a more common goal oriented atmosphere is formed. As the Bass theory implies, "a strong emphasis placed upon trust will increase human satisfaction in terms of feeling of accomplishment and as the center of gravity in relation to successful leadership", (1999). Becoming a successful leader, is accomplished through *trust* between leaders and subordinates, *commitment* to the team and organization as a whole and to some degree, *leader actions*. *Trust* and *Commitment*, as it pertains to the *Intent to Leave,* were shown in this study as statistically significant and in fact strengthen the findings of both Milligan (2003) and Vadell (2008).

Trust is a person's belief that someone or something is reliable, good, honest, and effective; it's the belief that one is capable of performing duties in a certain manner to attain mission accomplishment. It is believed that our personalized ideas of trust affect our personal interactions. Bass's Theory of Leadership tells us that the extent to which a leader is transformational is measured in terms of influence on the followers. The followers of transformational leaders feel trust, loyalty and respect for the leader and because of the qualities of the transformational leader are willing to work harder than originally expected. These outcomes occur because the transformational leader offers followers something more than just working for self-gain; they provide followers with an inspiring mission and vision and give them an identity. Trust lies at center of this theory and emphasizes the importance of the role of observational learning and social experience in the development of not only subordinates but leaders possibly even more so!

Understanding how to foster the development of trust is a vitally important goal because it can lead to living a more productive and cohesive team, not matter the size or the mission.

The Department of Defense has looked into this trend of transformational leadership as style for the military in order to step-up for future challenges, technological advances, and an increase of operations throughout the world. As the U.S. Army continues to increase the operational stride throughout the world, trust seems to be a developing factor in relationships between leaders and their subordinates. As previous scholars have suggested, trust as a key to "successful organizational outcomes including cooperative behavior, reduced conflict, improved communications, effective crisis response and improved performance" (Milligan, 2003, p. 155) in the military. Due to a continued Force Reduction Board through FY16 and a certain future decrease of junior officers, increased operational footprint and the increasing conflict with ISIS, the following conclusions of the study:

*Trust* is a growing factor in leadership and captain's leaving the Army. According to the research, there is a significant relationship between *trust* and *intent to leave*. This study suggests that with decrease in *trust*, there will be an increased *intent to leave*. According to the research there is a strong relationship between *commitment* and *intent to leave*. As mentioned in Milligan's study (2003), this signifies that officers' with a stronger sense of duty and an obligation to the Army are less likely to leave after their initial term of service. As mentioned in Vadell' study (2008), this signifies that officers' with a stronger sense of duty to the military are less likely to leave the after their commitment.

This research found that with an increase of *trust* in leadership there will be a decrease of captains leaving the Army. As the Army reduces its active duty numbers, the possibilities of reducing the turnover in the Army due to trust may improve. The study found that with an increase of trust in leadership there will be a subsequent decrease of initial term captains leaving the Army. If trust is in fact directly related to a captains intent to leave the military, further efforts of gaining the much needed trust in service members should be at the forefront of the Army in addition to making it on one of the five characteristics of the profession. An ever more serious approach may be to gage the senior leaders over evaluation based off of a level of trust they instill within the group they influence. That may be a truer measure of trust which may weed out the toxicity within the senior leaders in the Army.

Although the literature on trust is neither prevalent nor specific to any of the military organizations, it speaks directly to the transformation strategy outlined in the 2014 Quadrennial Defense Review and validates the significance of studying trust in a military organization. The U.S. military is rapidly changing to a downsized force with a higher rate of operations around the world. The employment of new technologies, have all changed the dynamics of military leadership, resulting in a wider span of control and a need for increased trust, teamwork and collaboration, all of which, as the research shows are dependent upon, influenced by, and made possible by trusting in leadership.

Limitations

The study had limitations mainly because of the study population and held bias to the inclusion criteria of only those in the rank of captain, due to the needs of the research. Without this limitation the research would become too broad of a research. The incremental value of looking at this narrowly defined segment of the U.S. Army population sample serves as a useful piece in building a lasting profile of the factors impacting retention strategies. While recognizing that the five military services are separate and unique an establishment, this research assumes that prior research into one of the other services is relevant and applicable to the U.S Army. This research also assumed that while the mission of the military organization is different, there is enough similarity in interpersonal issues, leadership issues, and organizational issues to make organizational research conducted outside a military environment relevant to military organizations. Given the complexity of the study variables, survey methodology and measurement may be limiting and therefore may not reflect in totality the attitude of the respondents. The research failed to offer respondents an opportunity to report deeper feelings and attitudes regarding the study variables. Additionally, some participants displayed a reluctance to admit a lack of trust, commitment, leader actions since they are attending the premier institution and serving commensurate with their rank in the Army.

The research literature suggested that trust is a fundamental ingredient to successful leadership. Prior research presented data suggesting that trust is key to successful organizational outcomes including cohesive behavior, reduced conflict, improved communication, effective crisis response and improved performance Vadell (2008). In a military environment, where the success of leadership is often a life or death outcome, trust is a force multiplier and the "glue" that bonds together the cohesion, leadership, and training, all which are preconditions for the consistently successful execution of warfighting doctrine (Shay, 2000).

Delimitations

The boundaries of this study were restricted to captain (junior officers) in the United States Army. The delimitation of other ranks is necessary in order to focus solely upon how the study affects captains at this critical juncture of their career. If this limitation was not established, this research would have been considered too broad and would not hold true in the measure of the untended population. The value of viewing this limited and defined Army population of captains offered a useful piece of the puzzle of gaining insights on factors having an impact upon retention strategies at different military ranks.

## Significance

This study advances the field of trust in military leadership, especially in the U.S. Army, on the premise that certain behaviors that one adheres, influence their perceptions of leadership. The officers in the Army rely on leadership performance and trust in order to carry out daily missions which support the higher headquarters mission, subsequently supporting the nation's defense. Although the literature on trust is not specific to military organizations, it speaks directly to the strategy outlined in the 2014 Quadrennial Defense Review and validated the significance of studying trust within a military organization. This study advances the field, especially in the U.S. Army, on the premises that certain leadership qualities and factors attribute to a heightened level of subordinate trust for senior leadership. The significance of military leadership is that military retention, may in fact, be an overall function of leadership's ability to gain the trust of their subordinates.

## Recommendations for further research

Several areas are rich for further research to better understand, build and sustain trust of the Army Profession. Research efforts need to assess and track the trust relationship among Army leader and subordinates as the institution transitions from a deployed force at war to a regionally aligned, home station-based force, even as we continue with operations around the world.

The results of this research suggest three areas for additional studies. The first area regards the narrow the sector of the Army used in this study. Given the relationship of trust in leadership, commitment, leader actions, with intent to leave the military, does the same relationships apply to the enlisted forces? Does prior enlisted service have an impact of trust in leadership? Making up the enlisted force is the Noncommissioned Officers, the backbone of the Army. Is there a level of trust in leadership that demonstrates a relationship in the enlisted Soldiers' role of trust in leadership? Is there a relationship between their role of trust in leadership, commitment, leader actions, and the intent to leave the Army? Is trust gained more in the enlisted force than in the officer realm? Is the same senior leadership affecting the intent of the enlisted members leaving the military? The current study placed a limit on the scope of military personnel used in the study and was not able to research the role of trust in leadership within the enlisted realm. Further research between the relationships of junior offices in this study compared to those in the enlisted force may prove beneficial, specifically if prior enlisted service make a statistical significant difference.

The Army was the only military branch chosen in this research. The Army, Air Force, Marine Corps, Navy, and Coast Guard have similar rank structures, and further studies may explore the role of trust in leadership within different branches. Cultural differences between each military branch may demonstrate a relationship or difference in the role of trust in leadership, commitment, leader actions and the intent of leaving the military service. Because leadership is different in various military branches, is there a similarity of trust issues in leadership present? The current study supplies enough evidence to portray this in the Army. Can it be assumed that there are similar issues in different branches? Further research is needed to compare the different branches with respect to the same issues as current operation tempos increase.

Researchers should evaluate the effectiveness of professional military education systems to develop Army leader competency with regard to strategic management. They should conduct and publish empirical studies, drawing on academic theory to contribute to senior service college curricula. Such topics necessarily include strategic decision making, strategic force development decision process analysis, and strategic management to support national strategy-policy interfaces. Findings in this research are such that there is enough statistical evidence to state that an exploration of the relations of organizational commitment in the military is needed. Is the military going to need more officers' in the future, as the operation tempo is increased? Is the military preparing to take actions as the numbers leaving the military increase? How is leadership addressing the issue of organizational commitment within the unit? Do leaders with prior enlisted service gain more respect and trust than those leaders without prior enlisted service? A further study in military environments within a single or multiple branches may be needed to help organizational and trust issues in the military.

Additionally, the Management Behavior Climate Assessment is the only available instrument that has been demonstrated to measure trust in leadership. While the MBCA is found to be extremely reliable, efforts to improve the construct validity need to possibly be undertaken to include attempts to shorten the MBCA. Some of the CASCOM participants in this study revealed a high level of unwillingness to participate in lengthy survey due to inundation of academic requirements and the perceived repetition of survey questions. Lafferty (2003) found core items that loaded directly on the consistency and credibility factors, using these core items, a shortened version of the MBCA should be developed and validated.

Vadell (2008) and Milligan (2003) both suggest that there is still much to be learned about commitment and its consequences for both work related and non-work related outcomes and that the military is an extremely valuable resource for increasing understanding of the work attitudes of military members as well as for the field as a whole. The findings in this study suggest that additional research into organizational commitment in military populations is needed. Will the low commitment levels found in this study be repeated with a similar organization a few years down the road? If so, what other organizational outcomes are being impacted by low levels of commitment? Are there measurable efforts that the DOD can implement to address low levels of commitment? How exactly might leadership practices enhance levels of trust and commitment? Further study in military environments may shed light on these important organizational trust issues.

Final comments to leadership on retaining quality junior officers

Retention of junior officers, especially captains, has been and remains a critical challenge for the Army. The Army has a considerable investment in these young leaders. Many of the causes for their early departure are documented in this research. Trust in leadership and the overall command climate are both basic contributory factors related to the many issues that result in early departures of quality officers. The leaders on the ground at all levels are the "hands on" experts who through continuous dialog and communication are able to keep officers and their families content enough to retain them, yet trust in the military leadership continues to be a growing concern.

The Army should implement as policy a series of evaluations and inspections during the last month of a commander's tour aimed at assessing the actual status of the unit. Such an evaluation should include focus group discussions and one-on-one interviews by evaluators. This inspection philosophy should validate the long-term status of personnel and unit overall readiness as well as levels of morale.

Lastly, officers who choose to depart the Army conduct exit interviews with their losing unit, the results of which are held at the unit level. A recommended course of action would include an Army-level holding of those exit interviews or the administration of exit interviews at the Army level, with results to those interviews made public for future research and analysis. Such a repository of information could greatly enhance officer retention studies, the results from which could feed directly back into leader recruitment and development efforts.

REFERENCES

Allen, N.J., & Meyer, J.P. (1996). Affective, continuance, and normative commitment to the organization: An examination of the construct. *Journal of Vocational Behavior, 49,* 252-276.

Allison, P.D. (2001). *Missing data.* Thousand Oaks, CA: Sage Publications.

Anderson, J.A. (2005). Trust in managers: A study of why Swedish subordinates trust their managers. *School of Management and Economics*, 14(4), 392-404.

Angle, H.L. & Perry, J.L. (1981). An empirical assessment of organizational commitment and organizational effectiveness. *Administrative Science* Quarterly.

Albrecht, S., & Travaglione, A. (2003). Trust in public-sector senior management. *International Journal of Human Resource Management, 14*, 76-92.

Asch, B. & Hosek, J. (2000). *Military Compensation Trends and Policy Operations.* Santa Monica, CA: Rand.

Aubrey W. D. (2013) Operationalizing the Construct of Toxic Leadership in the Unites States Army, University of Pheonix.

Babbie, E. (1998). The practice of social research (8th ed.). Belmont, CA: Wadsworth.

Bass, B.M., & Avolio, B.J. (1994). *Improving organizational effectiveness through transformational leadership.* Thousand Oaks, CA: Sage Publications.

Bass, B.M. (1998). Transformational Leadership: Industrial, Military, and Educational Impact. Mahwah, New Jersey. Lawrence Erlbaum Associates.

Boon, S. D. and Holmes, J. G. (1991). The dynamics of interpersonal trust: resolving uncertainty in the face of risk, in: R. A. Hinde and J. Groebel (Eds) Cooperation and Prosocial Behavior (Cambridge: Cambridge University Press).

Brockner, J., Siegel, P. A., Daly, J. P., Tyler, T. and Martin, C. (1997). When trust matters: the moderating effect of outcome favorability, Administrative Science Quarterly, September, p. 558.

Burns, J. MacGregor, (2010) Leardership, Harper Political Classic, (1st edition).

Chief of Staff of the Army Leader Development Task Force Report, (2013) http://www.usma.edu/scpme/siteassets/sitepages/home/csa%20ldtf%20final%20 report%2006213.pdf

Clegg, C., Unsworth, K., Eptiropaki, O., & Parker, G. (2002). Implicating trust in the innovation process. *Journal of Occupational and Organizational Psychology, 75,* 409-422.

Conger, J.A., Spreitzer, G.M., & Lawler, III, E.E. (eds.) (1999). The leader's change handbook: An essential guide to setting direction and taking action. San Francisco: Jossey-Bass.

Cooper, D.R., & Schindler, P.S. (2006). Business research methods (9th ed.). New York: McGraw-Hill.

Covey, S.R. (1991). Principled-centered leadership. New York: Simon & Schuster.

Dirks, K. T. & Ferrin, D. L. (2002). Trust and leadership: meta-analytic findings and implications for research and practice. Journal of Applied Psychology, p.628.

Doney, P.M., Cannon, P., & Mullen, M.R. (1998). Understanding the influence of national culture on the development of trust. *Academy of Management Review.*

Drechsler, D. Charles, A. (2008). Why senior military leaders fail - And what we can learn from their mistakes; Air Force Journal.

Fairholm, G.W. (1994). Leadership and the culture of trust. Westport, CT: Praeger Publishers.

Feinberg, B.J., Ostroff, C., & Burke, W.W. (2005). The role of within-group agreement in understanding transformational leadership. *Journal of Occupational & Organizational Psychology,* 78(3), 471-488.

Field, 2009 Discovering Statistics Using SPSS, 3$^{rd}$ Edition, London. Sage

Frutiger, Russell Lloyd (2002). Unified leadership and organizational climate within American military services: Eliminating the roadblocks to true jointness. Ph.D. dissertation, Walden University, United States -- Minnesota. Retrieved May 5, 2012, from ABI/INFORM Global. (Publication No. AAT 3068414).

Greenleaf, R.K. (1970). *The servant as leader.* Indianapolis, IN: The Robert K. Greenleaf Center.

Greenleaf, R.K. (1977). *Servant leadership: A journey into the nature of legitimate power and greatness.* New York: Paulist Press.

Hagel, Chuck, (2104). New York February edition: Pentagon Plans to Shrink Army to Prewar Level, pg. A1.

Halpin, Stanley, M. 2011. "Historical Influences on the Changing Nature of Leadership within the Military Environment." *Military Psychology* 23, no. 5: 479-488. *CINAHL Plus with Full Text*, EBSCO *host* (accessed April 26, 2012).

Hannah, S. T., & Avolio, B. J. (2010). Moral potency: Building the capacity for character-based leadership. *Consulting Psychology Journal: Practice and Research, 62*(4), 291-310. doc: 10.1037/a0022283

Hannah, S. T., Avolio, B. J., & May, D. R. (2011). Moral maturation and moral conation: A capacity approach to explaining moral thought and action. *Academy of Management Review, 36*(4), 663-685. doi:10.5465/AMR.2011.65554674

Headquarters, Department of the Army, 25 November 2009. "A leader development strategy for a 21st century Army," 1. Washington, DC: Headquarters, Department of the Army.

Kipnis, D. (1998). Trust and technology. In R.M. Kramer, T.R. Tyler (Eds). *Trust in organizations: Frontiers of theory and research.* Thousand Oaks, CA: Publications.

Kouzes, J.M., & Posner, B.Z. (2002). The leadership challenges (3rd ed.). San Francisco

Lafferty, C.L., Wagoner, C.W., & Levin, S.L. (1999). Organizational trust in an Air Force Reserve squadron: An inquiry using the Management Behavior Climate Assessment. Proceedings form the Conference on Human and Organizational Studies. George Washington University: Washington DC.

Leedy, P.D., & Ormrod, J.E. (2001). Practical research: Planning and design. Upper Saddle River, NJ: Merrill Prentice Hall.

Levin, S.L. (1999). Development of an instrument to measure organizational trust. An unpublished doctoral Dissertation. George Washington University: Washington.

Likert, R. (1967). The human organization. New York: McGraw Hill Publishers.

Luhmann, N. (1988). *Familiarity, confidence and trust: Problems and alternatives. In Bambetta, D. (Ed.), Trust: Making and breaking co-operative relations.* Oxford: Basil Blackwell, 94-107.

McAllister, D. (1995). Affect and cognitive based trust as foundations for interpersonal cooperation in organizations. *Academy of Management Journal, 38,* 24-59.

Mayer, R.C., Davis, J.H., Schoorman, F.D. (1995). An integrated model of organizational trust. *The Academy of Management Review, 20* (3), p. 709.

Mathews, J. (2006). Leader relations model: An alternative approach to the traditional process of leadership. *The Journal of Business Perspective, 10*(4), 37-48.

Meyer, J.P., & Allen, N.J. (1996). Affective, continuance, and normative commitment to the organization: An examination of construct validity. Journal of Vocational Behavior, 49, 252-276.

Milligan, P. K. (2003). The impact of trust in leadership on officer commitment and intention to leave military service in the U.S. Air Force. Dissertation Abstracts 1-179. (UMI No. 3123495).

Mobley, W.H., Horner, S.O., & Hollingsworth, A.T. (1978). An evaluation of precursors of hospital employee turnover. Journal of Applied Psychology, 64, 408-414.

Mowrer, O. H.: "Q-technique"-description, history and critique. In O. H. Mowrer (Ed.), Psychotherapy Theory and Research. New York: Ronald Press, 1953, pp. 316-375.

Northouse, P.G. (2001). *Leadership: Theory and practice* (2nd ed.). Thousand Oaks, CA: Sage Publications, Inc.

Northouse, P.G. (2004). Leadership: Theory and practice (3rd ed.). Thousand Oaks, CA: Sage Publications, Inc.

Odierno, R. T. (2012a). Feb. 9, 2012 -- Gen. Raymond T. Odierno remarks to House Army,www.Army.mil/article/73660/Feb__9__2012____Gen__Raymond_T__Odie rno_remarks_to_House_Army_Caucus_Breakfast/

Papasan, Jay (2013) The ONE Thing: The Surprisingly Simple Truth Behind Extraordinary Results Hardcover. April 1, 2013, #1 Bestseller.

Parra, L.F., & Smith, P.C. 1998. The relation between job level and job satisfaction. Group and Organization Management, 23: 470-495.

Perry, R.W. & Mankin, L.D. (2007). Organizational trust, trust in the chief executive and work satisfaction. *Public Personnel Management*, 36(2), 165-179.

Thomas Ricks, "Younger Officers Quit Army at Fast Clip," *Washington Post*, 17 April 2000, A1.

Rotter, J. B. (1980) Interpersonal trust, trustworthiness, and gullibility, American Psychologist, January, pp. 1–7.

Sashkin, M. (1996), Management Behavior Climate Assessment. Unpublished manuscript, The George Washington University, Washington, D. C.

Sashkin, M, Levin & S. L. (2000). Development of an instrument to measure organizational trust. Unpublished manuscript, The George Washington University, Washington, D.C.

Schlosser, P. Robert. (2003) Officer Trust in Army Leadership, University of Oklahoma

Shamir, B., & Ben-Ari, E. (2000). Challenges of military leadership in changing armies. *Journal of Political and Military Sociology, 28 (1),* 43-60.

Shay, J. (2000). *Preventing Psychological and Moral Injury in Military Service.* www.belisarius.com/modem_business_strategy/shay.tp. Retrieved March 2003

Snider, Don. M. *Once Again, The Current Challenge to the US Army During a Defense Reduction: To Remain a Military Profession* (Carlisle, PA: Strategic Studies Institute, 8 February 2012).

Spitze, James Moffat, and Judith J. Lee. 2012. "The Renaissance CIO Project: THE INVISIBLE FACTORS OF EXTRAORDINARY SUCCESS." *California Management Review* 54, no. 2: 72-91. *Business Source Complete*, EBSCO*host*

Steele, Anneliese, M. Are The Relationships Between Junior and Senior Leaders In The U.S. Army Officer Corps Dysfunctional? A MONOGRAPH, (2001) CGSC Fort Leavenworth, KS, School of Advanced Military Studies.

Stephenson, W.: Introduction to inverted factor analysis, with some applications to studies in orexis. J. educ. Psychol., 1936, 27:353-367. Stephenson, W.: The Study of Behavior. Chicago: University of Chicago Press, 1953.

Tan, H.H. and Tan, C.S.F (2000). Toward the Differences in Trust and Supervisor and Trust in Organization.

Vadell, Jamie. (2008) The Role of Trust in Leadership: U.S. Army Officers' Commitment and Intention to Leave the Military. Capella University.

Weber, M. (1947). The theory of social and economic organizations (T. Parsons, Trans.). New York: Free Press. (Original work published 1915)

Wojak, Adam (2010) "Is Experience the Missing Link in Junior Officer Development?"

CONSENT LETTER

JUN 2015

Dear survey participant,

      Hello, I am a doctoral student at Trident University, studying trust in leadership in the U.S. Army. In this study, I hope to achieve a baseline for a better understanding of leadership and its impact on military retention of junior officers. Potential benefits of this study include a better understanding of the level of trust that exists between senior leaders and Army captains and how that may impact a decision to remain in the Army or to seek alternative employment. I hope you agree that both knowledge and learning are critical to change and agree to complete this survey.

      Your participation in this survey is completely voluntary; I offer no incentive for participation. Your decision to participate will not affect your position at the Captains Career Course. You are not being asked to report on the level of trust of any one individual leader, rather your observation on the level of trust between military leaders and subordinate officers. Responses will be kept strictly anonymous. No personal identifiers are associated with this survey. Do not write your names on them. Surveys are numbered for data processing purposes only. I am the only person with access to them.

      If you have questions regarding this research feel free to contact my dissertation chair, Dr. Pamela Wilson at, Pamela.Wilson@trident.edu, or the Institutional Review Board at Trident University International, 5757 Plaza Drive, Suite 100, Cypress, California 90630; Telephone: (714) 226-9840.

      I look forward to receiving your responses and sincerely appreciate your participation in this study. Congratulations in advance on your upcoming graduation from the course!

Respectfully,

John A. Forsyth
john.a.forsyth.mil@mail.mil

**Demographic Survey**

Please circle your response

1. What is your Military Occupational Specialty (MOS)?
   a. Combat     b. Combat Support     c. Sustainment

2. What is your total combined number of deployments Iraq or Afghanistan?
   a.  0          b.  1 - 3        c.  4+

3. What is your ethnic background?
   a.   African American
   b.   White Caucasian
   c.   Other _____

4. What is your education level?
   a.   Bachelors
   b.   Masters
   c.   PhD

5. How many years of service (YOS) have you served in the U.S. Army?
   a.    1-4     b.  5-10     c.  11+

6. What is your gender?
   a.   Male     b.   Female

## Management Behavior Climate Survey

Please mark your response with an X in the box to the right

| | In the U.S. Army, senior leaders... | Rarely / Never | Seldom | Occasionally | Usually | Almost Always |
|---|---|---|---|---|---|---|
| 1 | are consistent in their dealings with different people. | | | | | |
| 2 | tell the same story to each person that they speak to. | | | | | |
| 3 | "stay the course" and persist over time in the actions they have decided on. | | | | | |
| 4 | maintain the same viewpoint tomorrow as they express today. | | | | | |
| 5 | disclose relevant information. | | | | | |
| 6 | report strategies that accurately describe the course of actions they took. | | | | | |
| 7 | act the same tomorrow as they do today. | | | | | |
| 8 | act to keep their word. | | | | | |
| 9 | say today what they will make happen tomorrow. | | | | | |
| 10 | respect the trust they are given. | | | | | |
| 11 | don't play favorites. | | | | | |
| 12 | say the same thing to different people regardless of the circumstances. | | | | | |
| 13 | act in a consistent manner over time, even in different contexts. | | | | | |
| 14 | express themselves in a consistent way from one time to the next. | | | | | |
| 15 | present important information accurately. | | | | | |
| 16 | take responsibility for the errors as well as credit for accomplishments. | | | | | |
| 17 | speak accurately of what they will do. | | | | | |
| 18 | keep their promises. | | | | | |
| 19 | state outcomes that actually occur. | | | | | |
| 20 | tell the truth. | | | | | |
| 21 | treat strangers as fairly as they treat friends. | | | | | |
| 22 | avoid telling different people what they want to hear. | | | | | |
| 23 | behave in a way that does not contradict prior actions. | | | | | |
| 24 | describe the same way, today, what they reported yesterday | | | | | |
| 25 | do not censor relevant information. | | | | | |
| | | | | | | |

| | In the U.S. Army, senior leaders...<br><br>Please mark your response with an X in the box to the right | Rarely / Never | Seldom | Occasionally | Usually | Almost Always |
|---|---|---|---|---|---|---|
| 26 | accept responsibility for what they have done. | | | | | |
| 27 | act as they said they would. | | | | | |
| 28 | by their actions, demonstrate respect for commitments they have made. | | | | | |
| 29 | make sure that what they say will take place actually takes place. | | | | | |
| 30 | do not lie to suit their purposes. | | | | | |
| 31 | reject requests for special treatment based on friendship. | | | | | |
| 32 | adhere to a consistent statement, regardless of who they speak to. | | | | | |
| 33 | act in ways consistent with their past actions. | | | | | |
| 34 | don't change their story to fit the context. | | | | | |
| 35 | are open with relevant information. | | | | | |
| 36 | accurately report information about their past actions. | | | | | |
| 37 | do what they say they will do. | | | | | |
| 38 | deliver on their commitments. | | | | | |
| 39 | make realistic predictions. | | | | | |
| 40 | act in a trustworthy manner. | | | | | |
| 41 | treat opponents as courteously as they treat supporters. | | | | | |
| 42 | tell different people the same thing. | | | | | |
| 43 | follow through with actions consistent with their statements. | | | | | |
| 44 | report what they will do in the same terms when they have done it. | | | | | |
| 45 | openly share important information. | | | | | |
| 46 | provide correct information about prior behavior. | | | | | |
| 47 | carry out actions they have said they would take. | | | | | |
| 48 | follow through on promises. | | | | | |
| 49 | accurately state future outcomes. | | | | | |
| 50 | can be trusted. | | | | | |

# Continuance Organizational Commitment Survey

| | Please mark your response with an X in the box to the right | Strongly Agree | Moderately Agree | Slightly Agree | Slightly Disagree | Moderately Disagree | Strongly Disagree |
|---|---|---|---|---|---|---|---|
| 1 | I would be happy to spend the rest of my career in the Army. | | | | | | |
| 2 | I am afraid of what might happen if I left the Army without having a job lined up. | | | | | | |
| 3 | I think people move from company to company too often. | | | | | | |
| 4 | I enjoy discussing the Army with people not on active duty. | | | | | | |
| 5 | It would be hard for me to leave the Army without having a job lined up. | | | | | | |
| 6 | I do not believe that a person must always be loyal to their organization. | | | | | | |
| 7 | I feel as if the problems within the Army are my own. | | | | | | |
| 8 | Too much in my life would be disrupted if I decided to leave the Army now. | | | | | | |
| 9 | One of the reasons I continue serving in the Army is that I believe that loyalty is important and therefore feel of sense of moral obligation to stay. | | | | | | |
| 10 | I do not feel a part of the Army Family. | | | | | | |
| 11 | Right now, staying in the Army is a matter of necessity as much as desire. | | | | | | |
| 12 | If I had another offer or better career opportunity, I would not feel it was right to leave the Army. | | | | | | |
| 13 | I do not feel emotionally attached to the Army. | | | | | | |
| 14 | I feel that I have too few options to consider leaving the Army. | | | | | | |
| 15 | I was taught to believe in the value of remaining loyal to one organization. | | | | | | |
| 16 | The Army has a great deal of personal meaning to me. | | | | | | |
| 17 | One of the few serious consequences of leaving the Army is the scarcity of available alternatives. | | | | | | |
| 18 | Things were better in the days when people stayed in one organization for most of their careers. | | | | | | |
| 19 | I do not feel a strong sense of belonging in the Army. | | | | | | |
| 20 | One of the major reasons I stay in the Army is that leaving would require considerable personal sacrifice – another organization might not be able to match the overall benefits I have here. | | | | | | |
| 21 | I do not think that wanting to be a "company man" or "company woman" is sensible anymore | | | | | | |
| 22 | I think that I could easily become attached to another organization as I am to the Army. | | | | | | |
| 23 | It would be too costly for me to leave the Army now. | | | | | | |
| 24 | Jumping from organization to organization does not seem unethical. | | | | | | |

| | Intent to Leave Survey    (Please circle your answer in each block) |
|---|---|
| **1.** | **Which statement most clearly reflects your feelings about your future with the Army in the next year?**<br>a. I definitely will not leave.<br>b. I probably will not leave.<br>c. I am uncertain.<br>d. I probably will leave.<br>e. I definitely will leave. |
| **2.** | **How do you feel about leaving the Army?**<br>a. It is very unlikely that I would ever consider leaving the Army<br>b. As far as I can see ahead, I intent to stay with the Army.<br>c. I have no feeling one way or the other.<br>d. I am seriously considering leaving the Army.<br>e. I am presently looking for other jobs and plan to leave the Army. |
| **3.** | **If you were completely free to choose, would you prefer or not prefer to continue working with the Army.**<br>a. I prefer very much to continue working for this organization.<br>b. I prefer to work here.<br>c. I don't care either way.<br>d. I prefer not to work here.<br>e. I prefer very much not to continue working for the Army. |
| **4.** | **How important is it that you spend your career in the Army rather than some other organization?**<br>a. It is very important for me to spend my career with the Army.<br>b. It is fairly important<br>c. It is of some importance<br>d. I have mixed feelings about its importance.<br>e. It is of no importance. |

| | **Intent to Leave Survey**<br>**(Place an X in the appropriate box to the right)** | **Strongly Disagree** | **Disagree** | **Agree** | **Strongly Agree** |
|---|---|---|---|---|---|
| **5.** | I am actively looking for other careers outside the Army. | | | | |
| **6.** | I will remain in the Army after my current commitment. | | | | |
| **7.** | I often think about leaving the Army because of too much time spent away from home. | | | | |
| **8.** | I intend to leave the Army because of too many deployments. | | | | |
| **9.** | If another organization offered me a job now, I would leave the Army, even if the salary were equal to my present salary. | | | | |
| **10** | As soon as my commitment is complete, I will leave the Army. | | | | |